MANY THINGS UNDER A ROCK

MANY THINGS

DAVID SCHEEL

ILLUSTRATIONS BY
LAUREL "YOYO" SCHEEL

YOUNG READERS EDITION

UNDER A
ROCK

THE MYSTERIES
OF OCTOPUSES

NORTON YOUNG READERS
AN IMPRINT OF W. W. NORTON & COMPANY
INDEPENDENT PUBLISHERS SINCE 1923

For Peyton and Robyn, who are always with me.

Adapted from Many Things Under a Rock: The Mysteries of Octopuses

For information about permission to reproduce selections from this book, write to Permissions, W. W. Norton & Company, Inc., 500 Fifth Avenue, New York, NY 10110

For information about special discounts for bulk purchases, please contact W. W. Norton Special Sales at specialsales@wwnorton.com or 800-233-4830

Manufacturing by Versa Press
Book design by Hana Anouk Nakamura
Production manager: Delaney Adams

ISBN 978-1-324-01999-2

W. W. Norton & Company, Inc., 500 Fifth Avenue, New York, NY 10110
www.wwnorton.com

W. W. Norton & Company Ltd., 15 Carlisle Street, London W1D 3BS

1 2 3 4 5 6 7 8 9 0

CONTENTS

Octopus Cognition

Solitary Octopuses

Society Octopuses

MANY THINGS UNDER A ROCK

A L E U T I A N

I S L A N D

Amchitka

Anchorage

Tatitlek

Cordova

Chenega

Prince William
Sound

Cook Inlet

Port Graham

Copper River

THE INNER LIVES OF OCTOPUSES

Underwater in Prince William Sound, Southcentral Alaska

I FOLLOWED THE OCTOPUS INTO THE EMERALD VOID BETWEEN THE surface and the depths. Above us, in sunlight, the water sparkled with glassy plankton. Below us the light vanished in darkening green over the flats just out of sight.

I swam parallel with the octopus, finning hard to match his pace. The octopus was a large juvenile male of perhaps twenty pounds and missing his second right arm. He jetted backward through the water mantle-first, arms trailing, until he pitched his body downward and we descended. He neared the bottom at a depth of about forty feet and abruptly turned white. He spread his arms and web wide, then grabbed hold of some kelp. His skin changed to the color of the kelp, and he pulled a broad blade over his head.

"I have disappeared," he seemed to say.

Yet he was still quite visible. His arms and the back of his mantle remained outside the cover of the kelp. I lowered myself as close to the bottom as I could in my bulky dive gear, pressed my cheek down, and peeked under his chosen shroud. A black horizontal pupil gazed back, lid slightly lowered, horns of folded skin raised in papillae over each eye. On noting me, one arm curled across the eye as though he didn't want me to see him, hiding there but not hiding well.

At that time, I had barely begun training as a scientific diver, and I was new to octopuses. I left him then and headed up to the surface, to air, light, and warmth. I was curious about everything I had seen, from the backward swimming posture to the changing colors, the missing limb, and perhaps most of all that hidden eye peering from under the kelp, peering out from behind his own suckers.

Underwater off Amchitka Island, Aleutians, Alaska
Giant predatory beasts live in the cold, remote depths of the Bering Sea. One of these was watching me.

Even in July, the waters around Amchitka were only 41 degrees Fahrenheit, and I was glad my scuba dry suit was keeping me warm. I was surrounded by canyon walls plastered up to ten inches thick with hard algae in shades of rose and baby pink. Green sea urchins dotted the narrow seafloor between, and sponges jutted out from the concreted walls and canyon floor in stalks and balls and towers.

Stands of tightly bunched *Alaria* kelp rose here and there, small blades near the bottom and long stipes leading up to the floats and larger fronds at the surface. Everything that wasn't rigidly attached swayed with the waves above.

At the surface, thirty-five feet up, an inflatable skiff tossed on the waves. I had plunged out of that skiff, a thousand miles from my home in Anchorage and two miles from our mothership (the research vessel *Norseman*), into the Seussian landscape below.

I was in unfamiliar territory.

It was my second day in the Aleutians, fifteen years after my earliest diving experiences in Prince William Sound. My dive buddy and I had come to one of Alaska's most remote and challenging environments to answer a simple question: was the local marine environment radioactive?

The United States had detonated three nuclear bombs at Amchitka Island in the 1960s and early 1970s during underground testing. The final five-megaton explosion, buried over a mile below the surface, had caused a seismic shock of nearly 7.0 magnitude. Were any radioactive materials leaking through cracks in the bedrock out of those deep test holes from forty years ago, materials that could contaminate the kelp, urchins, and predators of the Aleutian marine ecosystem?

I looked overhead as my dive buddy approached. The bag we had tied on the anchor line was now stuffed to the size of Santa's sack with kelp we had collected during the dive for later study. Tugged by the bag and line, the anchor banged and scraped on the hard bottom as the boat tossed in the chop above.

We were nearing the end of our air, and it was time to surface, when my dive buddy pointed over my shoulder. Her eyes were wide, bubbles clattering in alarm from her scuba regulator. I turned to look.

The head of a large octopus was rising slowly up over a nearby ridge. A thick arm slithered over the ridgeline, moving toward us and the anchor. Behind the advancing arm, the head of the octopus rose ever higher.

How big was this animal anyway? She looked huge and appeared to be growing larger as each additional sucker was revealed. The anchor clattered on the rocks some more. We were ringing a gong, and an ocean giant had answered.

"We don't find octopuses very often," I had earlier been told about diving in the Aleutians. "But when we do, they're big! The octopuses come to investigate the sound of the anchor clanking on the hard bottom." This story was a bit surprising. At the time, scientists believed that octopuses were "probably not deaf." But what they could hear, how (what organ functioned as ears?), and why were questions that had not yet been studied. We now have a better understanding that octopuses—and their relatives, the cuttlefish and squid—do respond to some ocean sounds that are detected by organs that, like those in our inner ears, also help regulate balance and sense changes in movement.

When I began my career, octopuses already were known as solitary animals, indifferent to each other except as threat or prey, and as cannibals with limited ability to recognize their fellow beings.

My curiosity was as strong as ever. Had that first octopus encountered years ago been embarrassed to be found? Octopuses are supposed to be good at hiding. Could an octopus feel embarrassed?

What interest could this second octopus, out in the remote Aleutians, have in the sound of metal banging on rock? What source of food or mates made a noise like that? I could think of none. What was really going on when a giant octopus answered the call of a clanging anchor?

Over my twenty-five years studying octopuses, I remained curious about how they live and experience the world. They cannot tell us how they feel, however, and they are worlds different from mammals, including from humans. Some believed that for these reasons it would be impossible to learn about the inner lives of octopuses.

That picture is changing. Over my professional lifetime, people have built, discovered, and learned new scientific ways to understand the experiences of animals. These have led us to discover previously unknown aspects of octopus physiology and previously unknown species, habitats, and behaviors.

One route to knowing others is also the most obvious. Behavior reveals values—what is good and what is bad to an octopus—and hints at an animal's experiences and intentions.

In *Many Things Under a Rock*, we will try to better understand the inner lives of octopuses. This is a story of what we have learned and what we are still learning about the natural history and lives of octopuses.

PART I
WHERE ARE THEY?

MISSING OCTOPUSES

1

STARTiNG OUT iN ALASKA

I MET MY FIRST OCTOPUS IN CORDOVA, IN SOUTHEASTERN ALASKA, in the new lobby aquarium in the US Forest Service building. Ophelia had arrived there in a bucket, brought by the fisherman who pulled her, entangled with kelp, from the muddy Copper River Delta.

In the lobby aquarium tank, she bobbed her head up and down at my peering round face. Without any change of her attention, two of her rear arms sought backward in the aquarium and found a gap under a rock. These two were followed by another arm, and she soon poured the rest of her into the same gap, from where her eyes still looked out. In a moment, the eyes also disappeared into shadow. The tank looked empty.

I came back on several other days to visit. I never saw her again, although she was still in the tank. Somewhere. A few months later the Forest Service brought her to the new Alaska SeaLife Center in Seward. She became their first octopus, an ambassador of her kind to people curious about life in northern seas.

When I first moved to Cordova, I frequently felt as though I were navigating unfamiliar waters. I had never lived on the coast; I was not comfortable on or near the water; and I had no experience with boats, salt water, fisheries, or underwater animals.

The bush town clings to a steep mountainside below Eyak Lake and above murky Orca Inlet.

At the town's feet, Prince William Sound begins, its deep, protected waters sheltered by islands and ringed by the retreating glaciers of the Chugach Mountains. The sound extends a hundred miles to the west. Moose wander through the yards of residents, shockingly tall next to cars and fences. Bald eagles perch on poles over the harbor. Outside my office window, I can see killer whales and wheeling mobs of seabirds that swoop and peck over the water. The town is not connected to an outside road system. Arrivals must come by boat, ferry, or plane.

Cordova Harbor is the briny heart of town, bursting with fishing boats. Alaska's fisheries alone support the careers of hundreds of fishermen and fisherwomen. Biologists monitor, count, and work to understand the populations of salmon, halibut, Pacific cod, and crabs that enrich these waters and drive Alaska's industry.

There is no commercial fishery for octopuses there, which means there is no one counting them, no one asking what they need to live and how they find it, no one funding researchers. In 1995, I could find just three biologists studying these octopuses, all their work done on their own time whenever they could. None lived or worked in Alaska.

Cordova sits on the traditional lands of the Eyak people, of Dënéndeh (Athabascan) heritage, and octopuses were important to the Eyak, Sugpiaq, and other Native peoples who live along the southern Alaskan shores. In Eyak, the word for octopus is *tse-le:x-guh*. Broken into its parts, it means literally "rock under many-dwell" or "many things under a rock." Because octopuses in that part of Alaska can often be found secluded under rocks at low tide, *tse-le:x-guh* is a wonderfully descriptive word, as the eight arms of a single octopus might properly be regarded as many things. For these people, octopuses were essential comfort food and part of their traditional way of life. This gave the octopus a place on the list of managed resources harmed by the oil spilled from the supertanker *Exxon Valdez* when it ran aground on Good Friday in March 1989. Some funding was therefore available at that time to better understand Alaska's octopuses as a harvested food source.

I had no experience in marine systems in Alaska nor with Native cultures. I was, however, trained to study animal behavior, eager to work, and already living in Alaska. My proposal was also the only one submitted for octopus research. I hoped to collect new data and to learn from elders of the coastal communities. Happily, I received the money I needed.

Forty miles northwest of Cordova, at the base of Ellamar Mountain, lies Tatitlek, a Sugpiaq village of about a hundred souls. Tatitlek is the village closest to where the *Exxon Valdez* ran aground. Millions of gallons of oil spilled in this disaster. Oil landed on beaches and damaged the health of marine animals. This severely limited the use of wild food sources by those living in Tatitlek and by Alaska Natives living in villages along more than a thousand miles of shoreline touched by the spill. In these villages, Alaska Natives introduced me to some of the places where they find their food. Giant Pacific octopuses (*Enteroctopus dofleini*) live in the waters of Alaska. In good years, they are an important food item harvested in coastal villages.

I asked in what kinds of habitats I could find octopuses. Those familiar with the cold, green waters of Prince William Sound told me octopuses are everywhere, in any marine habitat, and nowhere, seen only rarely. They told me that octopuses could not be studied.

I learned that many established scientific techniques used to study fish did not work well with octopuses. Octopuses are flexible, boneless, slippery, and elusive. They are also predators, which are relatively rare in nature. But while octopuses were hard to study, maybe it was not impossible to do so. The limited information, the old tales, and the warnings from locals stood as signposts, marking the edges of the unknown.

2

DANGEROUS GiANTS

I HAD PROMISED THAT I WOULD FIND AND CAPTURE OCTOPUSES IN Prince William Sound. Once captured, they could be weighed and assessed, their sexes and species identified and documented. These are the facts needed to understand animal populations and how they change. The part of this plan that worried me first was capturing the octopuses. Just how big would they be?

Giant Pacific octopuses, the species most often identified in Prince William Sound, grow on average to between thirty and sixty pounds at maturity, according to reports about this species from around Puget Sound and the marginal seas of Washington State and British Columbia.

But Gary Thomas, the Prince William Sound Science Center's president, told me about hooking a ninety-five-pound octopus while fishing for halibut. At the Cordova Historical Museum, I heard the tale of a diver who got too close to a big octopus, and it grabbed him by one leg. The diver was breathing surface-supplied air and connected to his boat by intercom, so he was not in danger of running out of air. The octopus held him underwater for two or more hours before he was able to free himself. I was not entirely sure these stories were true, but it still made me wonder. What sort of risk did I face in handling these wild animals?

The Eyak people tested themselves against these giants. Old Man Dude, a twentieth-century shaman "much feared" by the Eyak, told a story of two brothers who went out to hunt. They came to a place where the water grew murky and their canoe could not move at all. Beneath them, the water turned brown, and a huge devilfish emerged from the gloomy depths, swarming up to meet them. Its legs were as thick as dishpans. The two brothers strapped knives to their wrists and leaped into the water to do battle with the giant. They fought the devilfish until it died and floated up. It was 150 yards wide, and where it floated on the water, no one could paddle across it because the water was too thick with its slime.

Stories about octopuses of this size are hard to believe. Yet I found other reports of octopuses of similar size: there were too many stories to ignore.

An 1897 account from the Smithsonian Institution reported an immense dead octopus likely weighing several tons, but, as it turned out, the animal doesn't really exist. The Colossal Octopus entered the realm of science late in 1896 following a great storm, after which a decayed, damaged, and very large carcass lay on the beach south of St. Augustine, Florida. Like an octopus body, the largest part was sacklike, and there were numerous tendrils of flesh found around or still attached to it, giving the appearance of an astonishing octopus. Debate about the nature of this carcass began at once and continued for the next century.

In St. Augustine, Dr. DeWitt Webb examined the carcass and wrote to Professor A. E. Verrill at the Smithsonian Institution. Based on Webb's photos and notes, Verrill published a description of the animal. He named it *Octopus giganteus*.

Soon after, Verrill also received from Webb some tissue from the carcass. When he opened the package, Verrill realized he was wrong. The tissues "smell like rancid whale oil" and were largely made up of tough connective fibers. Verrill knew that the bodies of octopuses are muscular instead. He concluded the carcass was the remains of a whale and published a retraction of his identification of the carcass as a Colossal Octopus.

Using modern molecular methods, more recent reexaminations of the same tissue and tissue from similar specimens found later also identified those tissues as remains of whales or other familiar animals such as large sharks. This is the same conclusion Verrill had reached a century earlier using only his sense of smell.

With the Colossal Octopus out of the picture, was there still reason to fear the large size of giant Pacific octopuses? The stories made me wonder just how big they get. And how would I get into the water with them and work safely?

Our research team gathered for the first time in the Science Center conference room on a rainy afternoon in July 1995. Even though I had only been doing marine research for a few months, I was the expedition leader and responsible for everyone's safety.

I chartered a wooden trawler that had been converted into a research vessel named *Tempest*. Our expedition would consist of a science crew of six, plus vessel captain Neal Oppen and a single deckhand. My wife, Tania Vincent, was officially along as a volunteer researcher.

Dan Logan and Michael Kyte were our divers, with Neal as an alternate diver. Dan was a diver with a US Forest Service dive team. Michael had captured octopuses for the aquarium trade for more than ten years and was now a consulting marine biologist. Our two field assistants were Scott Wilbor and Kathleen Pollett.

Michael gave us a rundown on octopuses and how to handle them underwater. He briefed us on his methods and techniques for capturing them. He went over the basics of how to identify a den, how to approach from above and behind (so that the diver does not stir up silt and the octopus does not get agitated), and how to scoop up the octopus as it is moving out of the den, before it has a chance to grab hold of rocks.

"Once you've got it off the bottom," Michael continued, "then you can point it body-first into the bag and it will just glide right in. Now if we get a really big one," he paused, "you have to be a little concerned about letting the octopus get a hold of you. Even a medium-sized one is strong enough to pull your mask off or to take your regulator away."

In which case you could drown. A little concerning indeed.

"You can't really get into trouble unless the octopus is larger, in which case if it gets wrapped around you, it can pin your arms to your sides and you won't be able to retrieve your mask." Then Michael added, "Of course, that's not really serious, but if it has taken your regulator while your arms are pinned . . ." I began to understand Michael's sliding scale of trouble, although drowning with your arms free did not seem much better than drowning with them pinned.

"I'm sure we won't have any trouble," Michael said and looked around at the divers again. "But if we do, remember not to panic. Don't fight the octopus directly: collectively, its suckers are stronger than you are anyway, and it is too slippery to hold onto. Instead, pull an arm off one sucker at a time, like you would pull a bath mat off the bottom of the tub. If you're stuck, just let go and relax. The octopus may also let go and retreat."

When Michael talked about big octopuses, he meant somewhere in the range of 70 pounds or more. I wondered if we might find even larger ones in Prince William Sound. The verified octopus record was 156 pounds, captured just north of Victoria, British Columbia, in 1967. It measured almost 23 feet, from arm tip to arm tip. Accounts of octopuses weighing about 100 pounds are not that rare.

There are occasional reports of much larger animals, however. At the Santa Barbara Museum of Natural History, there is a photograph of a fisherman, Andrew Castagnola, with an octopus that he caught off Santa Cruz Island in 1945 with a stated weight of 402 pounds. In a second photograph in the same collection, another octopus caught off Santa Catalina Island looks about the same size, although no one weighed it.

Jock MacLean's reports from the 1950s top all claims for the species. MacLean was a commercial diver and fisherman who worked along Vancouver Island, British Columbia. Jock told many versions of his outsized catches over the years. In one tale, he captured a 437-pounder that "filled a forty-five-gallon barrel" and was weighed or measured. He also saw but never captured one giant that he estimated weighed 600 pounds and measured 32 feet across. However, in another version of the events, Jock captured several octopuses of around 400 pounds, and the 600-pound octopus was captured and weighed. Stories grow in the telling, and such estimates are highly suspect. All these weights are more than double the largest size noted in well-documented records.

Records for octopuses weighing 400 pounds or more all date from more than a half century ago. If such giants ever did exist, it is likely they are now of the past. And it is ironic that if such animals do still exist (assuming they ever did), they are not to be feared, nor battled and subdued. The last wild places on Earth are now so precious that even our half-mythical beasts and monsters would no longer be viewed as Terrors of the Deep but rather as marvels to inspire wonder.

Of all the places I have read about, the Puget Sound area seems to have the largest and most abundant octopuses. I hope to see a truly large octopus out on his daily rounds. If I do, I won't try to capture it and take it to the surface to weigh and measure. I will find some way underwater to estimate its size. Sure, my guess may be way off, and some critics might claim that it was not as big as I thought. But I won't mind; they won't have been down there with me, immersed in the story. They won't know what it really is like to glide through the water with half-mythical giants.

3

LOST HOMES

MY EARLY RESEARCH WOULD INVOLVE SCUBA DIVING, TO COUNT octopuses and study their habitats. But I also studied them on foot during very low tides, in the intertidal habitats that form where the ocean meets the land. My work, on land or sea, depended on my ability to locate an animal notorious for its ability to pass unnoticed. Finding octopuses was no less a problem than capturing and weighing them.

To learn how to see them, I went with Alaska Native elders harvesting octopuses along the shore. I started my fieldwork in 1995 with my assistant Scott Wilbor in the villages of Tatitlek and Chenega.

In Tatitlek, we were to learn from Jerry Totemoff, a serious Sugpiaq man of forty-five or so with short, dark hair. Jerry was the one who most regularly brought octopuses back to the village. I hoped that he would show us how and where he found them.

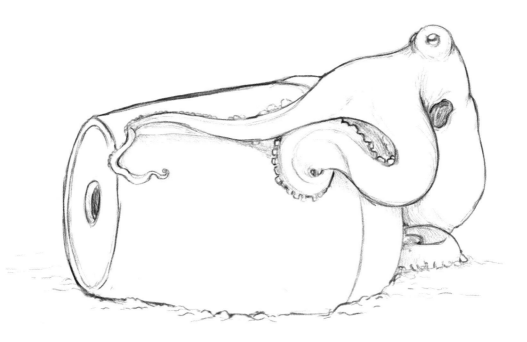

Soon after we
got to the Village Council office,
Jerry joined us. He wore XtraTuf rubber boots, the standard footgear
in this part of the world. He suggested we leave a half hour before
the low tide the next morning.

We met Jerry at 6:30 a.m. the next day, just as the tide went out
and uncovered the reefs we would be visiting. A light rain fell on the
quiet water of Tatitlek Narrows. The first outcrop of rocks was a few
hundred yards down a gravel beach from the Tatitlek dock. Along the
way, Jerry stopped at some alder bushes and cut off a five-foot-long
section of green branch, from which he stripped all the leaves and
smaller branches. On reaching the rocks, Jerry walked over them
to the seaward side and thrust his alder branch into a hole in the
rocks, probing for an octopus. I asked Jerry whether he had found
octopuses in this spot before.

"There used to be a lot of octopuses here, two or three every tide, but no more. Look here." He pointed to a hole in the rock, in front of which was a small spray of gravel with several small shells scattered over it. To my untutored eye, it was an unremarkable collection of debris from the beach.

"Nobody home," Jerry said. It wasn't until this remark that I recognized the hole for what it was: the entrance to an octopus den—the first one Scott or I had seen.

Just as people need lodging for the night, octopuses need shelter. In Prince William Sound, I would use the octopuses' need for shelter as a way to track them. The technique for finding an octopus with a green alder branch is simple. If the bottom of the hole feels hard, you are poking bare rock: the hole is empty. If the bottom is soft, on the other hand, there is something in there. But what? If it's a starfish, or mud, or almost anything else, then you can poke and prod and not much changes. But when you poke an octopus in its den, the indignant beast usually reaches out an arm to grab the intruder.

"What is this?" she wants to know.

When you gently try to remove the stick from the hole, she may hold on or pull it farther in, leading to a tug-of-war over who gets to keep the stick. The octopus usually tires of the stick when she decides she can't eat it. And often, having decided (correctly!) that someone is after her, she will retreat farther into the den. The next time you probe the hole, the stick will find only bare rock at the bottom.

Octopuses are picky about where they live. The shores of Prince William Sound and its underwater slopes are littered with rocks piled on top of sand or mud or more rocks, resting on bedrock, or forming boulder fields hundreds of yards wide. Yet most of these rocks are not suitable for octopus dens. I rarely encountered octopuses denning in or under boulders, unless they rested on mud, sand, or gravel, which would allow an octopus to dig a hole beneath the boulder.

Having found or built a suitable den, octopuses tend to return home each day to the same hole. If the resident moves out or is killed, another octopus may soon move in, so that over the years and decades the same holes turn up occupied again and again.

The intertidal dens we found almost always contained a pool of water. So even at low tide, the octopus sat curled up snug inside his or her own little homemade tide pool. When tides submerge the dens, the octopuses sit outside their dens, on the porch as it were, and watch the world go by.

These dens are wonderful hiding places. Only their midden pile—the ridge of pushed-up gravel, a few scattered shells—and a small opening mark the octopus's home. When in need of peace or safety, the octopus can slip inside, and only the slenderest eel-like predator can follow. Without hard outer shells for protection, octopuses are vulnerable to many predators, especially bottom feeders such as sharks, flatfish, seals, or sea otters. A surprise attack by a larger shark or otter can quickly overwhelm an octopus, but a den is a safe refuge. Once inside, an octopus is out of reach of almost any predator—even humans.

We were counting on Jerry to teach us to see the signs that octopuses left behind. And he was counting on our scientific training to learn more about the octopus population across the entire sound. He brought us to a rock outcrop located in several feet of water just off the Tatitlek dock. There were fewer holes here, but at one Jerry said, "I think somebody's home." We had found an octopus.

It weighed about seven pounds (three-and-a-quarter kilograms) and measured a bit shy of two feet (about half a meter long). I had worried that we might not find enough octopuses for our study to succeed, but when we found three more octopuses at another site later that day, my worries vanished.

By 10:00 that morning, the tide had risen, the reefs were underwater, and we were headed back into the village. Jerry dropped us off and left, giving Scott and me time to review our specimens and to prepare for our next stop—Chenega.

After thirty bumpy minutes in the air from Tatitlek, our plane touched down onto calm waters and taxied into the harbor of the village of Chenega. We found Mike Eleshansky, a sixty-year-old Sugpiaq man and our main contact, at the Village Council office. I introduced myself and reminded him of his plans to find us a place to stay.

Because Chenega was getting a new dock put in, all the lodging in the village was full of construction workers. Mike put his chin in his hand and mumbled "Let me think" every few seconds while we waited. Finally, Mike said, "You'll stay with us."

Mike was a kind host. Scott and I slept on cots placed in the pantry, next to Mike's freezer and beneath neat rows of canned vegetables, packaged foods, and bottles of Tang orange drink mix.

That evening, as we discussed where to search for octopuses, Mike seemed to appreciate our interest and our reliance on his knowledge to find good sites for our study. He was keen to go to Old Chenega if the weather was good. It was two hours away by skiff, and he had not been out there recently. Old Chenega was the original site of Chenega village, which was destroyed in 1964 by a tsunami following the Good Friday earthquake. About twenty years later, the village was rebuilt on another island twelve miles from the old site.

Before now, I had not heard about the earthquake from someone who had been through it. The quake hit at 5:30 p.m. on March 27 in 1964, reaching a magnitude of 9.6 and releasing almost twice the violent energy of the 1906 quake that nearly destroyed San Francisco. In areas around the sound, the ground rose and fell in undulating waves three to four feet high, creating rough seas of land. After the quake, huge ocean waves from the south swept away the village of Chenega. Survivors spent the night and the next day waiting for help, huddled and cold on a hillside above the wet slopes where their homes had once stood. Every survivor lost family to the water that day. Twenty-six people drowned from a village of about 120—meaning that more than a fifth of the population was lost.

The next morning we left the house at 6:00 a.m. to make the skiff ride to Old Chenega in time for the low tides. Mike stood at the tiller, squinting into the glare off the water, guiding us to his childhood home. As we neared Chenega cove, he pointed out the old schoolhouse, a weathered white building leaning into the hillside, as though the old building and the ancient island each held up the other during the recent years, abandoned to their fates.

Mike eased the throttle back and pointed to absent landmarks: where the dock had once stood, where the church had been. Then we beached the skiff and walked along the shoreline. Periodically, Mike would point out a prominent boulder, usually high up on the shoreline.

"We used to get 'em under that one."

We climbed up the beach to the rocks he indicated, but it was clear that each was too far from the water. Because of the 1964 earthquake, the land where we stood was around six feet (two meters) higher and fifty-five feet (seventeen meters) to the south of where it had been when Mike lived here. Like his own home, the octopus houses had been destroyed during the earthquake.

On that fateful Good Friday more than three decades past, the quake struck with no warning. In my mind's eye, I saw the people of the village as they might have been that March afternoon. The peace of the holy day was shattered by the distressed earth, which groaned and heaved and surged beneath their feet for several long minutes. Shelves tumbled off the wall in pantries, dumping cans and jars to the floor. Floors cracked. People were thrown from their feet. Buildings and trees swayed, and a loud roaring filled the air, even though there was little wind. Then, as suddenly as it moved, the island settled into its new position on the seabed. A brief quiet descended over the village.

Ten miles from Old Chenega, however, across an icy strait of water and up a long, narrow fjord, the earthquake caused a huge underwater landslide beneath a tidewater glacier. The glacier then disintegrated, sending tons of ice falling in a cataclysmic plunge into the sea. The waves created by the landslide and the crashing ice were funneled down the narrow fjord directly toward Chenega Island.

On the Chenega shore, the tide was already dropping. Waters receded with deadly silence to an unnatural low in the minutes following the quake. Children playing along the shore first noticed the empty seabed. Parents or uncles were already racing down the hill to call the children to higher ground, knowing that powerful waves were likely to follow the quake. As the children turned toward their parents' calls, the waters of the sound returned, racing up the beach with a deafening roar, tumbling boulders the size of houses in their path.

The first wave surged up the island slopes, pulling children from the hands of their fleeing parents as it swept ashore. Older children helping younger ones were lost in the swirling waters, which climbed higher and higher as the wave submerged the village. Then the second wave arrived, traveling fast and one hundred feet tall. It swept up boats, piers, and buildings, ripped trees from their hold on the land, and plundered life as it receded. The second wave smashed the village to ruins and swept the wreckage into the bay, filling it with broken houses and swamped boats. Yet a third wave rose and flooded the village again, after which the floating ruins had vanished without a trace. Survivors, fearing more waves, gathered higher up the hill beyond the reach of the water.

Like the villagers, the octopuses, too, had lost their shelters. As this small band of cold and grieving villagers huddled on a hilltop, gazing in the cold light of the full moon at the ruins below them, dozens of octopuses, maybe more, of all sizes crouched along the shore. They might have instinctively waited for the water to return in a few short hours with the returning tide. Others were left in the open, their boulders tumbled and dens destroyed like the houses of Old Chenega. But this time the receded water did not return. Octopuses too timid to move slowly dried out and died in the open or froze as the shallow pool of seawater in their transformed landscape drained away or turned to ice. Others crawled down the beach in the moonlight. But even these might not have fared well. On reaching the water, instead of the near-shore boulder field where they were used to finding many safe hiding places, they found a bare plain of silt and gravel.

We never did find an octopus that day on the shores of Old Chenega. The earthquake had lifted the octopuses' old houses up to the new tree line, and few new dens could be found along the current waterline. I thought about those octopuses back in 1964, and I hoped that, like Mike Eleshansky, they all arrived safe and sound at some new place to call home.

FiNDiNG OCTOPUSES

4

OUR COUSIN OCTOPUSES

Prince William Sound, Alaska

I KNELT ON THE ROCKS IN HIP WADERS. IN A SMALL TIDE POOL before me was a tiny octopus, one of the smallest that my shore team and I had found. Male octopuses lack suckers at the tip of the third right arm, but on this octopus, on that arm, two rows of tiny suckers continued all the way to the end. It was a female. From tip to tip, she was about as large as my hand, and she weighed only seventy grams, a little more than an extra-large egg.

This was our first expedition with divers. The dive team was prepared to encounter giants underwater. But this was the second tiny octopus the shore team had found on our beach walks. Could these little creatures really be the giant Pacific octopus we were expecting? Or were they another species entirely? Grappling with this puzzle would drag me in far-flung directions.

For the moment, the beach at Shelter Bay was deserted. The *Exxon Valdez* oil slick had poured into the bay six years earlier, coating and smothering the shorelines. Now, the waves and weather had scrubbed clean the hard, rocky beaches. Although oil still seeped from beaches in more than a few places around Prince William Sound, we did not see any sign of the spill here.

There were few suitable homes for octopuses. This was not the type of spot where we would come to expect them. Hard rock outcrops formed a point on the eastern shore of Shelter Bay, where

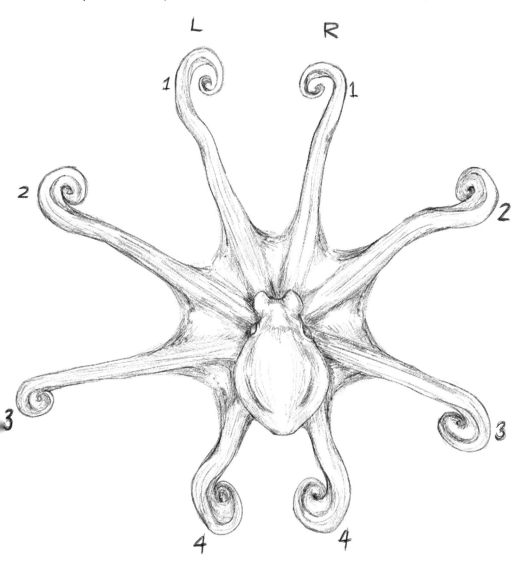

I now stood. We checked the crevices in the outcrops and looked for tide pools. There were no boulders under which to search.

We almost missed her. A bit of crab shell caught our eye as it lay in a tide pool no bigger than a kitchen sink, on a flat shelf of rock. A thin crevice ran through the rock above this pool. In the dark crack was our little octopus. After coaxing her out and taking her measurements, we put her back in her pool. I propped up a rock to protect her from the seagulls until the tide came up again to cover her.

Half an hour later, on our way back to *Tempest*, I stopped by the pool to see how she was faring. I tilted up the covering rock to peek, and there she sat, still looking exhausted from her ordeal with the biologists. Her arms curled in delicate spirals by her side, and her eyes were bright, but she did not react to my presence. Unlike other octopuses we released, she had not yet crawled back into her crevice, which was still above water.

Muted reds, tans, browns, and cream colors spread slowly across her head and mantle. Waves of color washed down one arm to pass out the tip and then reappeared at the base of the arm to sweep down again. This was my first sight of the dramatic color-changing abilities of cephalopods. The speed and flow of colors reminded me of the Alaskan northern lights.

More than three hundred different species of octopuses live along the world's ocean edges. And scientists continue to discover new ones. Still more species inhabit deeper waters. Due to the changing nature of their appearance, it is not simple to recognize each species. Despite this changeability, skin patterns are useful to identify the species of living octopuses, even though the identifying colors and characteristics for each species may not always be visible.

Many of these species have similar life cycles. Among the coastal octopuses, females tend their eggs until they hatch. There is no parental care after hatching. Some species, including the giant Pacific octopus, hatch into a life stage called paralarvae. These young hatchlings swim toward the surface to feed on the plankton. After some time feeding and growing, the paralarvae shift from swimming to clinging. They cling to debris or anchored algae, then move down to the ocean bottom as juveniles and dwell on the seafloor the remainder of their lives. We have found octopuses already living on the bottom that were as small as one-and-a-half grams, or about the weight of half a small

Suckers

Arms

Head

Eyes

Siphon

Gill Slit

Mantle

Mouth

Web

grape. At this size, they hide in shells, kelp holdfasts, and under rocks. Other octopus species have larger eggs, and the young live on the bottom immediately after hatching. Both types of coastal octopuses usually live alone, although there are exceptions.

Coastal bottom-dwelling octopus species have some characteristics in common. They have muscular, somewhat-spherical bodies and lack fins. At the center of the animal is the head, with high-placed large eyes and a downward-facing mouth. Inside the mouth is a beak, similar to a parrot's beak. Surrounding the mouth are eight arms, each with one or two rows of suckers on their undersides. A web of skin connects the arms. The octopus can spread its web wide like a net to capture prey or to make itself appear much larger than normal. Behind the head is the mantle, a muscular sac containing the body organs. The mantle inflates to draw in seawater through the octopus's gill slits, then expels the water through a tubelike funnel called the siphon. The octopus gets oxygen from the seawater flowing over the gills. The siphon can appear on either side of the head, emerging from the gill slit or underneath the animal. Most species also have ink sacs and can eject an ink cloud from the siphon when pursued.

Two important features identified living giant Pacific octopuses back in 1995: their large size and the wrinkles, or "extensive skin folds," on their bodies. So what were we to make of these tiny octopuses in Shelter Bay? Even giant octopuses begin as babies, but perhaps these small animals belonged to another much-smaller species. If we were finding very young octopuses, size would not help us identify them.

We needed to focus on the second trait: their skin. Octopus skin is textured and colored in patterns that change, and octopus species can be very similar to one another. But each species has some distinctive patterns that set them apart.

An octopus has a lot of skin. Take a giant Pacific octopus out of the water, and skin droops off its body like baggy, loose jeans. Put the octopus back in the water, and for a second those extra drapes of skin float around its arms and body like silk scarves. Then a remarkable transformation takes place. The skin tightens up and takes shape. Muscles beneath the skin can create textures ranging from small bumps to higher folds or ridges. These bumps—the papillae—help the octopus blend into the environment. Two papillae sprout like horns above the octopus's eyes, bringing to life the feature that earned them the old name of devilfish. The arms curl lazily in on themselves, forming neat little spirals that tuck against the web.

Glance away for just a heartbeat, then look back, and suddenly the octopus is lost against the background. If the octopus is in a patch of shotgun kelp, it may disappear entirely. Its reddish-brown skin matches the color of the kelp. The folds of loose skin mimic the rippled and swaying kelp fronds. No clear outline of an octopus remains.

But which of these appearances were uniquely specific to the giant Pacific octopus, and which might occur among other species? The internet did not yet have the many color photographs of octopuses that are available today. (Even now, many internet photos incorrectly identify the species.) Preserved specimens in museum collections were of little help, as distinctive skin patterns often only appear when the octopus is alive. We had to rely on descriptions in field guides and on drawings, not photographs, as we tried to identify these tiny octopuses.

We thought that the most likely other species would be the red octopus (*Octopus rubescens*), described as having skin with "small, pointed papillae." We compared this to the "large truncate papillae" for giant Pacific octopuses. But how "pointed" was too pointy to be "truncate"—to look like a bit was sliced off the top? However inadequate these descriptions, they did focus my attention on octopus skin as an important feature to study.

Distinctive skin has been important in the evolution of octopuses and their cephalopod kin. All cephalopods are mollusks: the clams, snails, and related forms. There are three features that separate squids, octopuses, and their relatives as a group from earlier cephalopods that appear in the fossil record. These modern forms lack an external shell, have greater respiration capacity, and have skin that changes color in complex patterns. Many of their predators use vision to hunt. But octopuses are masters of camouflage, using shape or color to hide, and a hidden octopus is a safe octopus. They can change color as fast as they can move thanks to their skin. No slow, chameleonlike changes for them. An octopus's skin is unusual among animals: the many pigmented cells that allow an octopus to change color are controlled by muscles, which in turn respond to the nervous system. That is how bands of color sped down the arms of the tiny octopus in a tide pool on the beach. Biologists have dubbed the behavior the Passing Cloud display.

Down the beach, Tania appeared from around the bend and waved me on. "Hurry up!"

I was only inches ahead of the rising tide. I gently lowered the rock back over the tiny octopus and wished her well. As I started slowly down the beach toward the rest of the day, I puzzled over which aspects of her skin display would help identify her species. It would take further research before I was able to determine that this small animal in the tide pool was indeed a young giant Pacific octopus.

To discover this and learn how to identify the octopus species I was finding and studying, I would have to travel to Seattle, Washington, to meet another species. In the Puget Sound Hall at the Seattle Aquarium, a different octopus looked out of the square tank. The octopus could look across the hall toward the city shoreline, and she also had a view into the briny depths of a truly large tank where rockfish swam. The hall was otherwise empty—just the rockfish, the octopus, and me.

Although clearly similar to the octopuses I had seen in Alaska, she was subtly different. But how exactly?

All the octopuses I had seen before in Alaska were of a single species, the giant Pacific octopus. But this creature in Seattle was the red octopus, the other species found in Southcentral Alaska. What set the two species apart?

That she was small was again of little help. Every giant Pacific octopus starts off tiny and must grow through juvenile stages until they outgrow even the largest red octopus. However, her skin was notably pebbly. I had never seen a similar display among the wrinkled folds of the giant Pacific octopus. And those familiar wrinkled folds were entirely missing here. The papillae emerging from this octopus's mantle were pointed, yes, but they were spindly—very narrow for their length. They were also distinctly different, now that I had seen them, from the broad papillae that arose like distant, snowcapped peaks along the mountain-range mantle folds of giant

Pacific octopuses. Under her eyes, where giant Pacific octopuses were entirely smooth, there were three small but less-spindly papillae like coarse eyelashes. This was another clear difference between the two species.

I moved around the tank on all sides to find the best spot to take pictures of this little red octopus. I startled her, and a lighter color band pulsed into place, wrapping from side to side across the football of her mantle. I'd only once seen something similar but much less distinct on a giant Pacific octopus.

I was now certain that we were not confusing the small giant Pacific octopuses we were finding in Alaska with this other species. The details of the skin were completely different and quite recognizable. I had learned to recognize the body patterns that identified the giant Pacific octopus, even when my "giants" were small.

Other octopus biologists were learning the same lessons in other ways. Octopuses were more often being kept in captivity due to improvements in aquarium science. And they were more often

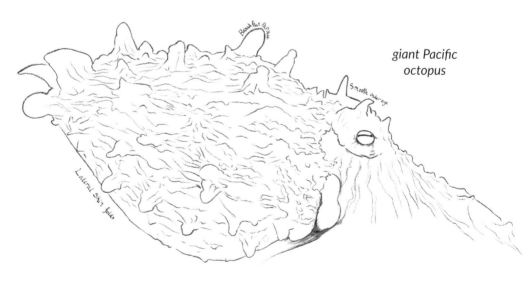

giant Pacific
octopus

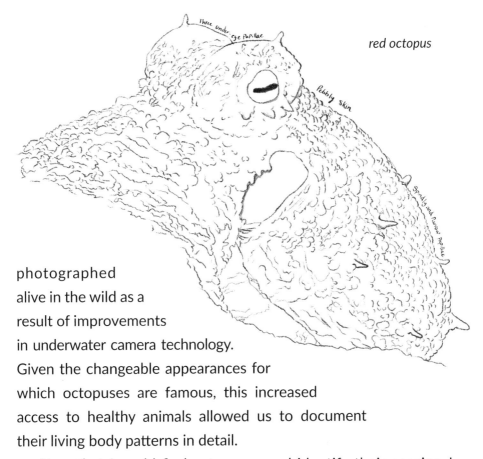

red octopus

photographed
alive in the wild as a
result of improvements
in underwater camera technology.
Given the changeable appearances for
which octopuses are famous, this increased
access to healthy animals allowed us to document
their living body patterns in detail.

Now that I could find octopuses and identify their species, I could begin to unravel another important question: what factors either limited or encouraged octopus population numbers?

5

OCTOPUSES OVERRUN

I CONTINUED TO WALK THE BEACHES OF PRINCE WILLIAM SOUND AT the lowest tides each year, counting octopuses and noting their sizes. While I worked, I wondered what determines the limits of a species' range? What controls their numbers?

A mother octopus lays many thousands of eggs. As the tiny hatchlings escape the eggs and drift as paralarvae in circulating ocean currents, we lose sight of where they came from and of what happens to them. The growth or deaths that influence their numbers along the shore could all be happening out at sea, where they are difficult to study and when octopuses are small and vulnerable.

Temperatures have direct effects on the fate of these paralarvae, speeding up or slowing down their growth. In the same ways, ocean temperatures also affect their prey and their predators. Cooling or warming ocean waters will even alter the ocean currents that carry the young octopuses from one place to another. These changes reverberate through food webs from the bottom-up, from the smallest algae using the energy of sunlight at the base of the food chain, up to the filter feeders or grazers and on to their predators.

As a result, the eventual arrival of many octopuses along the shore can be the product of distant or remote causes.

Winter 1899, Devon and Cornwall Coasts, England

A low-pressure weather pattern sat over the North Atlantic, resulting in southerly winds and milder winter waters off the coast of England. For those on the land, the warmer currents brought a wet and not particularly mild winter. For those in the sea, however, winter stayed farther north than usual, and its chilly grip did not penetrate to the south of England. In surface waters of the English Channel, Mediterranean octopus paralarvae thrived in the mild temperatures.

Late in May, a fisherman at Bexhill hauled up a crab pot and was surprised to find an octopus surrounded by empty shells instead of crabs. It was a big octopus, with a span about as long as the

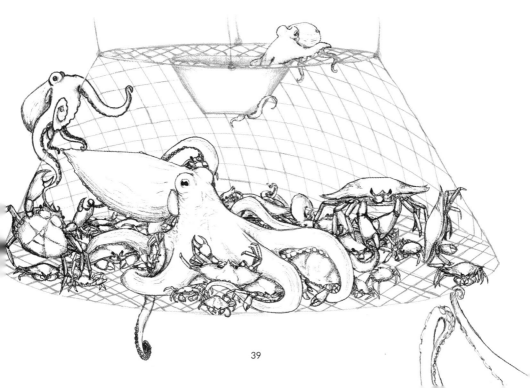

fisherman's arm. It had eaten every crab in the pot, and the empty crab shells would bring no money at the market. Still, the notable thing about this octopus was neither its size nor its appetite, but that this was the first one the fisherman had caught in thirty-five years working these waters.

By the middle of June, fishermen from Beer and Babbacombe complained about the octopuses taking crabs and lobsters from their pots. As the season advanced, fishermen were pulling up thirty or forty octopuses per day in their gear. Plymouth fishermen abandoned the shellfishery due to octopuses eating all their crabs and lobsters.

During August, octopuses entered Dartmouth Harbor in great numbers. They were larger now, having arm spans of four feet or more. Anglers in the harbor caught only octopuses on their hooks and lines.

In September, fishermen reported that very small octopuses were still plentiful south of Devon.

Octopuses remained unusually abundant throughout the next winter and well into 1901. By 1902, they were again scarce or absent on the coasts of southern England.

Nearly fifty years later, in 1950, the warm winter currents and octopuses in large numbers returned to the English Channel. In May, hordes of octopuses again decimated the shellfishery and remained through the summer and fall. This time, the plague lasted three years, through 1952, before notable declines occurred in the octopus population.

Spring and Summer 1982, Shimane Coast, Western Japan Sea
An abrupt warming occurred in the Japan Sea from May into early June. Argonauts sailed on these currents. The pelagic octopod

(*Argonauta argo*), also known as the paper nautilus or greater argonaut, lives offshore in tropical and warm temperate waters worldwide. This animal has a coiled shell and is a relative of octopuses.

In mid-June, large numbers of female argonauts were caught by Japanese fishermen using fixed set nets on the beaches, although argonauts normally were not found this far north. At times, a single haul of the net could bring in several hundred animals. Along with the argonauts, fishermen were hauling in unusually good catches of tuna, as well as young bonito, pilot fish, pompanos, and squid—all more tropical species associated with waters farther south. These exceptionally large catches continued until October in some parts of the country.

In these instances of the common octopus (*Octopus vulgaris*) along the southern coast of England and argonauts off Japan, unusually warm ocean currents caused the northward expansion of a species' range into new, usually colder areas where they were not normally found or at least not usually abundant.

The potential for a great leap in juvenile octopus numbers in shallow water always exists if weather and food sources are favorable, but that potential is nearly always diminished by the huge losses during the planktonic stage. A single giant Pacific octopus may lay more than a hundred thousand eggs. The large number is necessary because so many of the tiny hatchlings won't survive to become adults. Many will be eaten by predators; others will starve; still more will never reach a suitable habitat. For octopus numbers to stay the same, only two eggs out of those hundred thousand from one mother and her mate need to survive to reproduce themselves.

In rare years, however, the balance shifts in favor of paralarval survival, leading to abrupt increases in population.

When I started my octopus work, scientists understood a great deal about how temperature changes affect animal populations and movements. But over the decades, the effects of climate change on ocean lives would become clearer even to the general public.

MISSING OCTOPUSES AGAIN

6

GLOBAL OCTOPUSES

Cordova, Alaska

A LIGHT RAIN FELL FROM LEADEN GRAY SKIES ONTO STILL WATER AT the mouth of the Cordova Harbor. During my first summer of octopus work in 1995, every day's weather offered rain. Climate, on the other hand, takes a span of decades to see.

I rose from my desk and headed to the harbor. A few hours later, I departed aboard *Tempest* on that first diving and intertidal octopus expedition into Prince William Sound.

In that first year, I worried about how dangerous large octopuses would be and whether we would find enough animals to study. As I learned to cope with these concerns, I was more able to focus on the central questions of the work: Where were the octopuses? In what types of places did they choose to live? What controlled their population numbers?

Land animal populations are often limited by the number of top predators hunting down the food chain. In the ocean, however, animal populations, especially of invertebrates, are limited by algae growth that feeds up from the base of the food chain.

Plankton are small organisms that drift with the ocean currents. There are many different kinds. Phytoplankton are the very small algae and other life forms that convert sunlight into food using photosynthesis—in the same way that plants do. Zooplankton are tiny animals. Some are small their whole lives, while others, like octopus paralarvae, will grow into larger animals if they survive this stage of life. Most will be eaten by larger ocean creatures.

Two factors matter to those algae that make up the phytoplankton: sunlight and nutrients that are needed for growth. Sunlight in the ocean occurs in the surface water, of course. Little penetrates to the depths. But dead plants and animals containing nutrients eventually sink. These nutrients build up in deep bottom waters, which are too dark for photosynthesis. So sunlight and nutrients are available near

the surface only where and when coastal waters get well mixed. When those conditions are right, phytoplankton thrive, and swarms of zooplankton are able to feed off them.

In the long daylight of the Alaskan summer, the surface waters warm in the sun while fresh water from the land enters the sea at the surface. The warm, fresh waters float, while the cold, saltier water hugs the bottom. There is no force to mix the two. Early in the season, phytoplankton thrive on the nutrients in the well-lit surface waters. But by midsummer, once the phytoplankton use up the nutrients, new growth may stop.

In the fall and dark winter, the surface water loses heat rapidly, and storms mix the fresh water with the saltier water below, bringing nutrients to the surface. When the increased light returns in early spring, the wealth of waiting nutrients allows phytoplankton to thrive again. If the spring weather is calm, the surface will again run out of nutrients early. But when there is a windy and stormy spring, surface waters remain mixed later into the year, which creates a longer period of strong phytoplankton growth.

Greater numbers of phytoplankton support more zooplankton grazers as well as predators of those grazers—such as tiny, recently hatched octopus paralarvae. The paralarvae hunt the baby crabs that feed on the surrounding algae, and the more crab they eat, the faster the tiny octopuses grow.

In years when productivity at the base of the food chain is high, the phytoplankton capture the sun's energy and feed it up the food chain to larger plankton, and on to the fishes such as herring and Walleye Pollock that prey on the plankton, then even farther up the chain to large predators such as salmon, sharks, seals, and whales that feed on those herring and Walleye Pollock. When the cold waters rich with sufficient nutrients don't rise from the bottom, however, plankton are scarce, and the herring and Walleye Pollock must eat whatever they can find, including juvenile salmon and paralarval octopuses.

Temperature changes influence nutrients in these ways but also directly affect ocean currents. Shifting currents may bring greater numbers of zooplankton—such as octopus paralarvae—near the shores. As the small octopuses grow, they will soon settle to the ocean bottom from the waters above, looking for their next meal. These changing conditions may bring plagues of octopuses to the coasts of England, strand offshore argonauts along the coasts of Japan, or eliminate populations entirely.

~~~~~~

June 2004, Prince William Sound aboard Tempest
Nine years after that rainy, cold summer of 1995, the weather was warm during our annual survey expedition. The pitiless sun pressed onto the flat, calm sea. Those aboard *Tempest* jumped into the milky green water to cool down. The scuba dry suits that had kept us warm a decade ago now left us overheated on shallow dives in waters warmed by twenty hours of daylight in the near-Arctic summer. No one could remember such weather ever before.

I thought about the role climate played in the octopus invasions that had occurred in the last century in southern England. Those octopuses had been the common octopus, a species adapted to temperate and near-tropical temperatures that moved north in warm years.

Those twentieth-century invasions were advance warning of range shifts. By the first decade of the new millennium, the common octopus was found more frequently around the British Isles than in the Mediterranean Sea, where they lived before 1900. By 2090, under likely climate-change scenarios, this temperate species could be found around Norway and Sweden in the North Sea, about a thousand miles north of their homes before 1900.

The giant Pacific octopuses of Alaska are cold-water specialists. What effect will this warm weather have here?

At that moment in 2004 aboard *Tempest*, we were taking a short detour from our octopus-survey destination that was related to the warming temperatures. Our skipper, Neal Oppen, had spotted an iceberg. These came from nearby Columbia Glacier. Neal had to be on the lookout for any icebergs that lay in our route. Indeed, even as early as 1989, icebergs breaking off and escaping this melting glacier were a problem for ship traffic. This phenomenon contributed to the *Exxon Valdez* oil spill, as that tanker turned aside in part to avoid ice in the shipping lanes.

We were headed straight toward such an iceberg. Above the waterline, the ice was milky white, streaked with black lines and glinting in the sun. Below the water, the bulk of the ice showed shades of turquoise and aquamarine blue before fading out of sight. The chunk of glacier was as wide as *Tempest*. As we glided nearer, the ice loomed higher than the rails of the deck. Cautiously, looking below the waterline to see the size of the submerged ice, Neal slid us toward the motionless berg, still leaving plenty of space. *Tempest* came to rest more than one full iceberg-length away from it. "Ice can roll," Neal said, explaining the respectful distance.

He grabbed the twelve-foot-long boat hook and untied the small aluminum skiff. He pushed off from *Tempest* and, using the boat hook, pulled himself in the skiff toward the ice. Then he stabbed the berg, using the point of the boat hook to break off loose chunks of ice about the size of a microwave oven. Lifting the ice up on deck required the strength of two people leaning over the rail from *Tempest*. The gleaming frozen crystals had formed thousands of years ago from snow falling in the high mountains before beginning their long, slow slide down to sea level in a river of ice.

More ice was melting because our part of the world was warming. Warmer ocean temperatures restrict the mixing of the warmer surface waters and the colder bottom waters, while colder temperatures encourage mixing. Remember that well-mixed ocean waters encourage plankton growth. And in such cold conditions, octopus paralarvae grow quickly and then dwell more safely on the seafloor, and their sometimes-predators feast on other, more abundant prey.

Over the many decades since the emerging octopus swarms in southern England of 1900 and 1950, the planet has warmed—especially in the North Pacific. Giant Pacific octopuses seemed more likely to thrive in the cold, and from our perspective in 2004, these warming conditions did not seem favorable for them.

July 2020, the North Pacific

Warm temperatures broke records with dismaying regularity in Prince William Sound, the North Pacific, and around the world. Ocean environments for sea life are warming. Let's begin with March 2015, eleven years after we visited the melting glacial ice in 2004. In that month, over the eastern Gulf of Alaska and over the entire North Pacific, temperatures were the warmest they had been in the previous 136 years of recordkeeping. The year 2015 tied for the second-warmest ever recorded in Alaska, exceeded only by 2014.

In 2016, the 2014 record was broken. New records were set in 2018, 2019, and 2020. And in 2021, global ocean temperatures were the warmest in history, surpassed again in 2023, the warmest year around the whole globe (land and sea together) but also for the global ocean's average sea surface temperatures since records began in 1850. New records will soon be set. I was no longer finding octopuses in the sites I had visited for twenty-five years on the shores of Prince William Sound.

The Seattle Aquarium held a weeklong dive survey each winter in which volunteer scuba divers reported their encounters with octopuses and shared the reports with the public. The first such survey was in 2000. The aquarium was kind enough to share these data with me. I compared them to my own octopus counts beginning in 1995 and to publicly available temperature data.

I discovered that when octopus counts had been high, temperatures had been colder a year or two before. As the oceans warmed, octopus counts fell. This happened not just in Alaska but also for Puget Sound octopuses, too.

Warming waters resulted in fewer octopuses. The temperature effects on the octopus population likely occurred when each group were still paralarvae floating in the plankton. Warmer waters made it less likely for tiny paralarval octopuses to survive long enough to settle on the bottom and be counted.

For the giant Pacific octopus, as well as other octopus species, there is a thermal neutral zone. Temperature changes within that zone do not much affect octopus well-being. But once temperatures exceed this zone, even just one degree higher can cause octopus survival to fall by 15 percent, one study found. And with larger temperature changes, survival declined by 70 percent. Ocean warming is already shifting some octopus populations toward the polar regions, and continued warming will lead to dramatic declines in the near future.

In June 2020, I revisited our study sites, hoping to collect some octopuses for new research in the aquariums. I chartered a small floatplane. It was the first summer of the COVID-19 pandemic and because of social-distancing rules, I asked my children—the best octopus seekers in Alaska—to work with me. They had grown up combing the beaches for octopuses and were already part of my social bubble.

We headed out to Prince William Sound to visit the same beaches we had reached from the research vessel *Tempest*. With a smaller crew, I focused on bringing a few healthy octopuses back. However, I was to be disappointed.

We visited our two best beaches. In the early years, we had never missed finding signs of octopuses at these sites. In the latter years of our work, we were finding fewer octopuses, but their favorite dens were often still occupied.

In 2020, however, I was shocked to see almost no sign of octopuses at either site. On the first day, we found only one den that had been occupied sometime earlier in the year. There was no one home the day we checked. At the second site, we again found only a single den where an octopus had recently been. But again, there was nobody home.

Early in 2021, I was able to study a few more record-setting years of climate change to see how they impacted octopus counts drawn from reports of different divers in Washington State. These counts also showed fewer octopuses following warmer years, just as we had seen from the Seattle Aquarium reports and my own data in Alaska.

I began my twenty-five years of fieldwork in Prince William Sound with concerns about the spilled oil from the *Exxon Valdez* and its effects on octopuses and their habitats. I ended with similar worries about the effects on octopuses from climate change and the warming oceans.

7

OCTOPUSES SEIZED

ANDAVADOAKA IN MADAGASCAR IS A STUDY IN CONTRADICTIONS.
It's a coastal village that hasn't seen rain in three years. It's a place where cell phones are common but basic plumbing is not. And it's a village where reef gleaning, a traditional livelihood for women, now supplies harvested octopuses for sale in other countries.

Glimmers of dawn reach through five feet of slightly cloudy blue water. The seafloor below is scattered with bone-colored sand and patches of coral skeletons overgrown with brown algae. A curtain of net stretches out of view in either direction. The mostly empty net holds one dead Red Squirrelfish, only enough protein for at most a single serving. Farther along, the reef flat gives way to sand and eelgrass beds before the next reef section. As the tide falls and day brightens on that reef flat, an octopus awakens. Each of her arms alone has more meat than the entire squirrelfish. She is sheltered in a hole in the reef rock. There is no pile of food remains outside her den, only a small spray of unremarkable debris.

Above the octopus, a woman approaches on bare feet over the sharp reef. She is Vezo—those who make their living from the sea—a people who live along Madagascar's western coast. The reef flat is within their traditional gleaning waters.

The woman carries with her tools similar to the ones used by local people in Alaska to harvest octopuses for their food. She quickly captures the octopus from its den and kills it.

Her catch was a day octopus (*Octopus cyanea*), a medium-sized species found from the coasts of East Africa across the Indian and western Pacific oceans to Hawaii in the central Pacific. Artisanal fishers catch them to eat or sell them in commercial harvests. Octopuses may provide the only cash income for the Vezo woman's household.

Madagascar is one of the poorest countries in the world. Seventy percent of the Andavadoaka population make their living from the ocean. People here rely heavily on the sea for their food, their livelihoods, and their identity. The village, lying on the southwestern coast of Madagascar, gets little rain. The spiny forest surrounding the village is dry. There is no soil to grow food, just sand. Dry goods such as flour, rice, pasta, and lentils are brought in along the road. Fresh vegetables are scarce. Goats graze the dry vegetation and provide some dairy and meat, but most fresh food comes from the sea.

The reefs of Andavadoaka have declined in recent years and so have the species of fish that depend on them. On the fringing reefs along the shore, the effects of fish harvesting are apparent.

During recent decades, large fish became scarce. European Union and Asian commercial fishing ships have increasingly harvested tuna and billfishes offshore from these waters. As the international export market for octopuses and other fish has grown, the catch size and numbers have declined. Climate change and human population increases further threaten the nearshore marine systems that sustain the Vezo.

As the Vezo fishing community became aware of these declines in their harvests, they took action. They were helped by Blue Ventures, a British organization dedicated to sustainably improving food security in ways that make local economic sense. In 2004, traditional reef gleaners, frustrated by finding fewer and smaller octopuses, temporarily stopped harvesting octopuses in a part of their fishing grounds. They voluntarily protected their local marine areas. They named this management area Velondriake, "to live with the sea."

The good news is that day octopus numbers can recover quickly from harvest. This is a fast-growing species that can double in size in a little more than a month. Seven months later, when the Vezo returned to the temporarily closed areas of Velondriake, they discovered abundant and larger octopuses. The harvest was higher than it would have

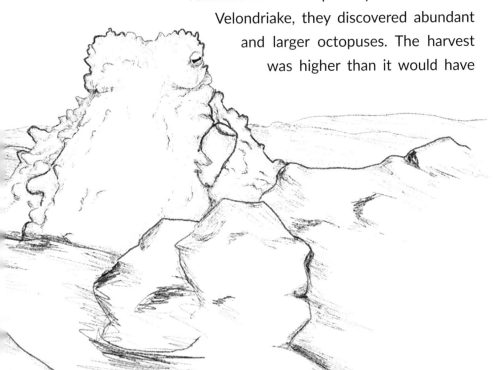

been without their intervention. The Vezo made more money than they would have if they hadn't given the octopus population the chance to recover.

By rotating the areas that they closed, they could let the octopuses grow while still harvesting and earning income in nearby areas that were not closed. Neighboring communities noticed the Velondriake success story, and a rotating schedule of temporary closures spread up and down the coast where octopuses were harvested and sold.

Predators can be beneficial to biological communities overall, and octopuses are no exception. Wherever octopuses thrive, as they do in the locally managed marine areas of Velondriake, the result is healthier fisheries and healthier reef communities. The common octopus could also have a role in protecting the health of the Mediterranean Sea, far from tropical Madagascar. Lionfish are predators that have invaded the Mediterranean after traveling from the Red Sea through the Suez Canal. And there are now a lot of them because they have no natural predators in the Mediterranean, leaving them to feast on the local fish populations, reducing their numbers. But in 2021, an octopus was seen wrapping a lionfish in its arms and web and subduing it, despite its large and venomous fin spines that make lionfish dangerous for most larger predators to attack. Could an abundance of wild octopuses, protected from harvest, help control the invasion of lionfishes? This is an example of the possible role of octopuses as predators in marine community health.

Because wild octopus populations can only sustain so much fishing, some people are trying octopus farming. Aquaculturists now raise hundreds of marine species in captive settings, from tuna to clams. Such cultivated products can make up half of the seafood market in some countries. Aquaculture octopuses may be promising, but the challenge is that octopuses do not appear suited to these forms of production.

Octopuses are carnivorous and enjoy eating the same marine creatures that humans eat—such as crabs, clams, and shrimp. While it's relatively easy to farm species that thrive on algae, it makes little ecological sense to harvest wild seafood to feed to octopuses and other carnivorous species.

Growing octopuses in aquaculture also would not be like caring for an octopus in a public aquarium—where the octopus is given space, diverse foods, and lots of engagement. Octopuses are very curious animals that thrive when given opportunities to explore and forage. They need these activities to be healthy and grow rapidly.

In aquaculture, animals must grow rapidly in crowded quarters. Most wild octopuses live alone, and they may even attack and kill each other when pushed into close quarters. Increasingly, scientists and the public are concerned about the welfare of all industrial farmed animals—both land- and marine-based species. That is one reason some people are turning to a vegetarian diet. Despite this, plans for the aquaculture of octopuses continue to move forward.

The challenges of octopus aquaculture make the management of wild octopus habitat and fisheries all the more important, particularly to small artisanal fisheries that help coastal communities thrive. As the Velondriake project demonstrates, protecting octopuses and their habitats through temporary closures by the Vezo resulted in both more octopuses and in more income from their octopus harvests.

PART II
WANT

TRACKING OCTOPUSES

8

OCTOPUS SCRAPS

Underwater in Prince William Sound, Alaska

THE FIRST SIGN WAS A SINGLE OVAL, ORANGE CRAB CLAW WITH black fingertips. It was from an Oregon rock crab (*Glebocarcinus oregonensis*) and just half the size of my pinkie fingernail. I followed a trail of small scallop shells and broken bits of crab up a slope to the base of a boulder, where I found the entrance to a den. The octopus was on top of the boulder with one arm wrapped neatly around a piece of kelp, watching to see if I would notice her. When I did, she jetted away.

I followed, swimming fast, determined not to lose sight of her. She broke to the right. My gaze followed, but she cast an ink cloud and turned sharply left. I pursued through the ink cloud and saw her dart into a patch of kelp. She froze. She turned translucent burnt sienna, the color of the brown kelps. Her skin roughened and became the texture of the kelp. My eye could only find her among the fronds if I focused on her suckers and her eyes.

Octopuses are perfectly camouflaged and well hidden in kelp or under rocks. But giant Pacific octopuses in Alaska also are messy and leave remnants of their meals behind. I found this octopus by tracking her scraps. In Prince William Sound, most midden piles left by octopuses contained remains of Oregon rock crabs more often than any other prey. Why is that what they have for dinner? Why was the world's largest octopus species so often choosing these small crabs?

Humans are omnivores, eating both plant and animal foods. Octopuses are carnivores, eating only animal prey. But are octopuses picky eaters?

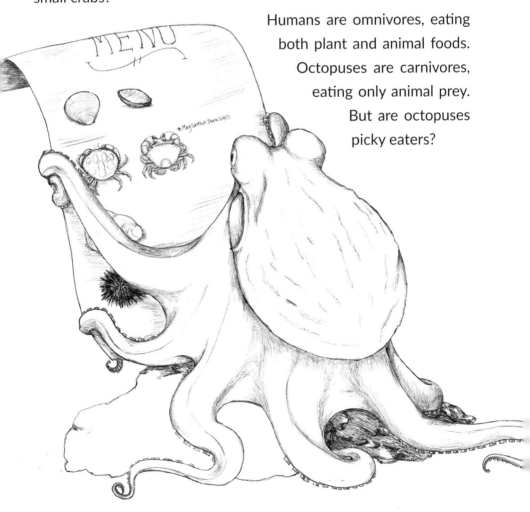

In Prince William Sound, midden samples that we collected over a period of twelve years revealed that octopuses eat at least fifty-two intertidal species, most commonly these little Oregon rock crabs.

Giant Pacific octopuses in other regions, however, captured a less varied diet of larger prey. In the Salish Sea of Washington and British Columbia, up to 80 percent of the diet was the large red rock crab (*Cancer productus*). In Aleutian waters, octopuses feasted on two large bivalves—the horse mussel (*Modiolus modiolus*) and the Alaska falsejingle (*Pododesmus macrochisma*), a relative of scallops—that together made up well over half their diet.

In Prince William Sound, most of the octopus middens consisted of remains from five smaller species. Oregon rock crabs made up 25 percent of their prey. The bigger red rock crab represented 20 percent, the large and speedy helmet crab (*Telmessus cheiragonus*) another 17 percent, the graceful kelp crab (*Pugettia gracilis*) made up 12 percent, and the black-clawed crab (*Lophopanopeus bellus*) amounted to 7 percent of the midden items.

Why did 81 percent of the diet of giant Pacific octopuses in Prince William Sound come from five smaller crab species, while octopuses in Saanich Inlet, British Columbia, ate just one species for the same percentage of their diet? And why did the Prince William Sound octopuses choose to eat the smaller Oregon rock crabs when there were more black-clawed and graceful kelp crabs on the beaches?

When we measured the sizes of the live crabs and the remains of the same species in the middens, we found that the crabs octopuses killed were bigger than the live crabs left behind on the beaches, typically larger by at least a third. Overall, octopuses liked to eat the largest of the species of crabs they could find and the biggest individuals within every species. Octopuses were picky. But why was the smaller Oregon rock crab preferred?

Crabs, it turns out, have parasites. In particular, the more common black-clawed crabs are susceptible to parasite infestation. We first realized this when we noticed an unusual number of black-clawed crabs appeared to be carrying eggs. But what we first mistook for eggs were actually the external reproductive organs of parasites. This type of parasite is a relative of barnacles, and it grows a rootlike system of filaments within the crab's body, feeding on healthy tissues. Infected crabs stop growing and do not provide as much energy as a healthy crab would when eaten. So by avoiding the infected crabs, the smart octopuses also avoided low-quality food.

Octopuses also avoided hairy crabs (*Hapalogaster mertensii*), which were rarely found in octopus middens. The meat of the hairy crab is as energy-rich as that of any other crab. They are also soft and slow and should have been easy prey. We don't know for sure, but perhaps the octopuses were not finding these crabs because they weren't foraging through the soft sediments under the rocks where hairy crabs prefer to live.

Crabs can avoid notice by octopuses, sometimes in elaborate ways. For example, the graceful decorator crab (*Oregonia gracilis*) hides in plain sight by covering its entire body with a collection of items such as algae, sponges, and anemones, along with the worms, brittle stars, or other animals clinging to these decorations. The ornaments disguise the crabs, and they go unnoticed unless they move. I found them many times hiding at the entrances to occupied octopus dens! The octopuses did eat them, but rarely.

Octopus middens also have remains from a variety of clams or other bivalves such as oysters, mussels, and cockles. Octopuses have also been seen dining on shrimp, whose shells are very fragile and light.

Octopuses even include odd or astonishing items in their diet. One day in 2012, pedestrians along the shoreline of Puget Sound noticed a Glaucous-winged Gull on the water in the shallows. The gull was acting strangely. Its head was underwater, but it was beating its wings on the surface. Around its neck was the red arm of an octopus. The gull flapped but to no avail. In a few minutes, the octopus had pulled the gull below and enveloped the bird in its web, leaving just the extended wing tips visible.

Brazilian researchers once watched a tropical octopus reach up from a tide pool to grab a Brown Noddy that had alighted on the rim. The octopus drowned the struggling bird and proceeded to feed on it over the next seven hours. The same researchers watched as a sally lightfoot crab (*Grapsus grapsus*) came within reach of a hidden octopus. In a fast grab, the octopus flung one arm from the water and caught the crab above. Another arm followed and ensnared the crab, and together the arms pulled it underwater.

Octopuses have quick, powerful arms with suckers anywhere along arms' length that stick on contact. Curiosity is built into the octopuses' anatomy. Like a human baby that puts whatever it finds into its mouth, an octopus investigates what it touches by passing it sucker-to-sucker toward the mouth. After all, it might be edible. The middens in Prince William Sound revealed curiosity of this kind. Octopuses were hunting large crabs but also sampling what the habitat had to offer. If something seemed interesting or edible, they tried it. Often that was a clam. Sometimes it was a spiky sea urchin, a slippery fish, or even feathered prey caught unawares.

We had an answer to our original question, "What food do giant Pacific octopuses choose?" Mostly here in Southcentral Alaska, they take the five crab species mentioned. They prefer the larger species and, within species, the larger individuals. In other locations, octopuses choose narrow diets of one or a few big species. But what accounts for this difference? Why are Southcentral Alaska diets more diverse, with smaller prey?

The answer seems to be that it depends on what food sources are available in each habitat. Our live prey surveys in Prince William Sound show that the largest prey are rare. At the northern edge of the range of giant Pacific octopuses, in waters forever changed by the massive *Exxon Valdez* oil spill, big meals are hard to find. Without big meals, octopuses catch the little stuff, the only food available. Even here, though, they continue to be smart and selective, taking larger prey and avoiding low-quality food.

This explains the "why" of the regional difference in octopus diets. In habitats with fewer large prey, octopus food choices have to be more varied for the hungry predators to get enough to eat. These answers raise new questions: What makes the hairy crabs unavailable or unappealing? How do prey species avoid or escape octopuses? And for that matter, how do octopuses recognize their prey?

To answer such questions, I needed to understand three things. How do octopuses defeat crabs and bivalves, which are the most heavily armored animals in the sea? How do the crabs try to thwart the marauding octopus? And what is the sensory world of the octopuses that allows them to detect and pursue a crab intent on escaping their suckered clutches? As it so happened, the nearly impenetrable armor of a defeated butter clam—strong enough, thick enough, and almost hard enough to resist attack—would show the way.

9

OCTOPUS TOOLS

*Shores of Port Graham, at the Mouth of Cook Inlet, Alaska,
within the Traditional Lands of the Sugpiaq*

HOW DID THE OCTOPUS DEFEAT THE CLAM? I PICKED UP THE LARGE shell. No other clam in this area grew as big as the butter clam (*Saxidomus gigantea*). The shell was nearly four inches in width, thick, and heavy in the hand—the strong armor of a well-protected animal. Yet an octopus had gotten inside. I'd picked up the shell outside an octopus den on a rocky beach.

How did the octopus get into this armored prey? No doubt, it had tried simply pulling on the large shell to pry apart the two halves. Octopuses have hundreds of suckers in two rows along each of their eight arms. The suckers are smaller near the mouth and arm tips and larger in between. Arms of the giant Pacific octopus bear about 115 sucker pairs or 230 suckers per arm, which works out to just under 2,000 suckers total. The male's third right arm, modified to pass sperm during reproduction, bears fewer suckers.

The suckers can hold with surprising force. Even one sucker gripping a human forearm can raise a small welt. Underwater, octopus suckers act like suction cups but can hold much more tightly than do the simple dome suction cups you might buy in a store. The suckers cling without effort to a surface even when the octopus is relaxed or asleep.

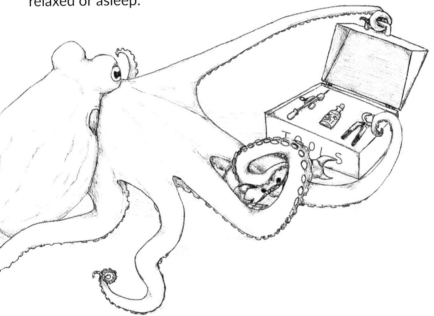

Octopus suckers adhere to anything they touch. I once gave Obi, a young day octopus, a toy to explore in her aquarium. The toy was a Mr. Potato Head, with pink ears, big red nose, eyes, and other body part pieces plugged in. I put a piece of shrimp inside the storage hatch in the potato's backside. The plastic potato was as large as the octopus.

Intrigued but cautious, Obi slowly stretched out an arm. Mr. Potato Head was not heavy and barely rested on the bottom. A sucker or two attached to the smooth plastic surface of the toy.

On contact, Obi pulled the arm back, startled. But the sucker didn't release, and so Mr. Potato Head moved toward the octopus. Obi, now detached, leaped back in alarm. Without the arm pulling on it, Mr. Potato Head drifted to a stop.

The sequence repeated, startling the hesitant octopus a second time. Still, this large and vaguely aggressive object commanded Obi's attention. On the third exploration, Obi approached with a threatening appearance—with her mantle darkly veined against a white background and her arms black except for contrasting rows of white spots. She made herself look larger by raising her front four arms above her eyes and spreading out her web along the arm edges. Mr. Potato Head missed the drama of this moment, as it had drifted face down and was staring into the sand. With her arms spread this way, lined with suckers ready to stop any escape attempt, Obi appeared larger than Mr. Potato Head, and her arms were now poised to engulf the toy.

Again Obi's suckers attached, and this large but light object approached her seemingly on its own. Obi's nerve failed, and she retreated nearer her lair. Mr. Potato Head drifted closer before coming to a stop, and she eyed it warily. She had yet to discover that the toy's various parts pulled out in tempting ways and that there was indeed a morsel of food hidden inside its hard but oddly lightweight shell. Obi was still exploring and learning with her suckered grasp about the behavior of light toys in captivity. She would later enjoy engulfing Mr. Potato Head in her web and removing its parts.

The giant Pacific octopus of Port Graham that had defeated the butter clam had taken the heavy bivalve in its suckered arms. But she was to learn the limits of her strength. With many suckers on multiple arms attached around both halves of the clamshell, the octopus no doubt had tried to pull open this armored prey, perhaps using some patience. Attaching the suckers requires no effort, but the octopus has to pull continuously with its arms to pry apart the clam halves, while the clam resists, holding itself closed.

With small clams, a giant Pacific octopus quickly and smoothly pulls the clamshell open, sometimes with enough force to break one side of the shell. But in the battle with this large butter clam, the clam proved too strong, and the octopus tired first. So the octopus tried something else. On the outside of the clamshell were no fewer than five separate marks, two marks on one half of the clamshell and three marks on the other side. Each of these showed an attempt by the octopus to get through the shell.

These tiny oval perforations are drill marks. Octopuses have a radula inside their mouths, which is a ribbonlike scraping organ they use to break up food and is lined with rows of microteeth. The radula begins the work of drilling into a shell and can make a hole by itself. But it cannot penetrate too deeply. Beyond that depth, the flexible salivary papillae, also tipped with scraping teeth, must take over. The salivary papillae send enzymes directly to the drill site that chemically weaken the shell, making it easier for the teeth at the papillae tip to wear it away. When the shell is finally penetrated, saliva is released through the hole, and its toxins subdue the prey, allowing the octopus to finally pry the shell open.

On the large butter clam, not one of the five drill marks made it through to the shell's interior. The octopus spent many frustrating hours in its den eroding these holes in the shell but always tired too soon or found that neither its radula nor salivary papillae could reach deep enough to get through. The wearied octopus started over each time in another spot. That shell was thick!

Five attempts to drill into the armor failed, yet the octopus still was not defeated.

On the rim of the clam, where the two halves met opposite the hinge, I found small marks that left a tiny gap to the interior of the shell. The mouth of the octopus contains a black beak similar to a parrot's. After a long battle using suckers and arms, radula and saliva, the octopus had defeated the clam by biting with its beak, finally chipping the edge of the shell at its thinnest point. Even though the chip was small, it exposed the inner clam flesh. This allowed the octopus to inject saliva that paralyzed the clam and weakened the connections between shell and muscle.

Many prey do not present the challenges of this heavy butter clam. We find many prey items with a single successful drill mark or a clear bite mark or ripped open by suckers and strength. Octopuses are well-equipped hunters with a formidable tool kit of body parts to defeat the heavy armor of their prey. They possess the curiosity to investigate, a fearsome patience in persisting to the end, and the flexibility to abandon one approach for another and another until the meal is won.

However, octopuses are not only the hunter. They are also the hunted.

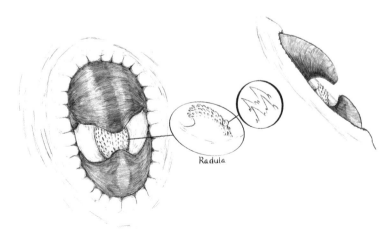

Radula

WATCHING OCTOPUSES

10

HiDiNG OCTOPuSES

I WAS UNDERWATER NEAR BUSBY ISLAND IN PRINCE WILLIAM SOUND, holding a yellow mesh bag containing an octopus ready to be released. With typical caution, the octopus reached two slippery arms slowly downward, interested in the rocks and open water in view outside the mouth of the mesh bag. The octopus was hesitant to move from the bag to a new place where dangers might lurk.

general resemblance using papillae

As I hovered over the bottom and waited for the octopus to exit, my dive partner tugged at my arm, gesturing. I didn't see what she was pointing to, but clearly she didn't want me to release the octopus at this spot. I looked around again through the shallow green water—nothing. My dive buddy shrugged.

Mottled pattern

We moved a small distance to where the edge of the kelp stands met the sand. At the base of a rock, I began again. Another tug on my arm—no, no! She pointed ahead, and we moved farther until we were directly above a thick understory of broad brown kelp, spreading into an unbroken canopy of blades just four to six feet over the bottom. Here, my dive buddy nodded. I began a third time to release the octopus.

Still unsure what had bothered my dive buddy, I was now more vigilant. She was the same. We faced one another, each peering over the other's shoulders into the murky waters, looking for anything that could pose a problem—stinging jellies, tangling lines, drifting dangers. I saw nothing. Facing the bottom, I opened the bag that contained the octopus. I sensed a shadow above me and looked up to see if my dive buddy was waving me off yet again.

Bold white stripe pattern

Instead, just inches from my mask and descending from above me was the large head of a curious juvenile Steller sea lion (*Eumeopias jubatus*), focused on the octopus meal soon to be released from the yellow mesh bag. For a brief moment I looked into her big, round brown eye. Noticing my awareness of her, with an easy flick of her flipper, she turned and was gone. Now I understood what my partner had seen. Our own clumsy diving activity had drawn the attention of a curious and hungry predator. Were we to release our octopus here, she would have little chance to use her camouflage skills to become invisible to the sea lion. We decided to release her the next day after the sea lion had left the area.

The risk of meeting these predators shapes the octopuses' world. Their first line of defense against predators is avoidance. Octopuses hide in their dens or crawl quietly through dense cover in search of their meals. They choose the largest crabs to keep their foraging brief. And they hunt for food at the time of day when their predators are least active. Then they usually return to the den, or another safe and sheltered spot, to open and eat their prey. This keeps them safely out of sight.

Octopuses can't always stay in their dens, though. Food and mates must be found. So the sensory systems of their predators have shaped how octopuses avoid being found.

The Steller sea lion as well as sea otters (*Enhydra lutris*), which are also common in these waters, are both mammalian predators. Mammals on land can use smells carried on the air to locate or track food. A few mammals, including otters that eat octopuses, are known to use smell underwater to hunt. A Eurasian otter (*Lutra lutra*) was filmed exhaling small bubbles from its nose and then sniffing them back in. The scents locked in the water bubbles dissolved in the otter's nasal cavity, leading it to a dead fish underwater in the dark.

This Eurasian otter species does not live in Alaska. The two otter species native to the United States are the North American river otter (*Lontra canadensis*) and the sea otter. It seems likely these species may use the bubble method to smell underwater, although no one has yet witnessed this for either species. Fish, rays, and sharks also may sniff out their prey in part by the chemical trails they leave.

In the tropics, day octopuses eat away from the den or carry remains of their meal some distance from the den before discarding them. Perhaps this makes their odors more difficult to detect. The moray eels that hunt them (unlike sea otters in Alaska) are able to enter an octopus den, if they can find it, and drag out an octopus. Moray eels are a constant danger to octopuses in the tropics. Although morays as a group are found worldwide, they reach highest diversity and abundance on tropical coral reefs. Moray species hunt at night and rely on scent to find their prey, although a few species forage visually.

Sea lions, however, might not be able to smell underwater, as they close their nostrils when diving. Hunters that use scent and are able to enter into a tight octopus den may be scarce in Alaskan waters. This may be why giant Pacific octopuses can be messy housekeepers. The remains from their meals don't draw predators to their dens because the predators can't smell them or aren't eel-shaped.

Mammals that become aquatic usually lose some sense of smell compared to their ancestors that lived on land. This includes the toothed whales and dolphins, whose ancestors were terrestrial. These marine mammals lack the olfactory part of the brain responsible for the sense of smell, along with related nerves. Aquatic reptiles, such as snakes, have also lost some but not all of their sense of smell. Sea snakes, many of which spend their entire lives in the water, have less ability to smell than amphibious snakes that live both on land and in water.

With the sense of smell absent or diminished, these marine

predators must rely largely on other senses. Hearing, touch, and vision are important. Whales and dolphins rely on sound and echolocation. Seals and sea lions can use their very sensitive whiskers to track the water movements left behind by fish as they swim along. And cephalopods use lines of pressure-sensitive cells along their upper arms and heads to sense movements in the water. Crawling octopuses do not leave swirling waters in their wake, though, so many predators also rely on sight to hunt.

In shallow tropical seas, the sun is bright and the water often clear. Vulnerable octopuses would be wise to hide in the daytime and to come out only at night. Yet this is the home of the day octopus, named because it is active during daylight. Day octopuses stay safe in a protective den at night to avoid nighttime predators such as moray eels that hunt by scent. But this puts the octopuses at risk from daytime predators that hunt by sight, including seals, sea lions, otters, birds, and many species of fishes.

Hiding in dens and under cover is the octopuses' first line of defense against visual predators. When they must go out, however, their second line of defense is hiding in plain sight by changing their appearance to look like something else instead of like an easy meal. The octopus is a master of disguise, a skill they use to fool visual predators.

Their first method of disguise is body color, which gives them two ways to hide the body outline. Octopuses can display on their skin large blocks, stripes, or bands of dark and light that a predator's eye sees as separate objects instead of as one octopus. The octopus may also use a mottled skin pattern—one with many colors, like a pile of autumn leaves or a pond frog's skin. The mottled skin matches the pattern of the gravel sea bottom where the octopus sits. The result is that it vanishes into the background. The color-changing system in the skin has several layers of different color or reflector cells. These are shown or hidden to create and change the octopus's displays and are controlled by nerves and muscles.

The second method of disguise is body texture. Octopus skin in a relaxed state can be smooth. But when in disguise, octopuses can raise bumps and spikes called papillae on their skin. They can also raise folds on their skin that will sway like kelp fronds or mimic other aspects of their environment, making the animal hard to see. The small-pointed papillae of the red octopus resemble the texture and color of small algae. The day octopus raises large, broad papillae topped with pale colors to look like coral tips catching the tropical sun. The coral reef and the octopus sitting atop it look the same.

The third method of disguise uses postures and movements. The octopus can pick a specific object nearby to imitate, such as coral, an algae stalk, or a rounded rock. It can then hold its body in positions that allow it to look like that object.

To the predator's eye, nothing stands out more than motion. The octopus takes advantage of this and tries to move like something other than an easy meal. To pounce on a crab or other prey, the octopus must spread wide its web and arms. Such an eye-catching movement cannot be hidden from an alert predator. But maybe the octopus can pull off a complicated trick, grab a meal, and live to eat it.

First, the web and arms blanch soft white, looking like a white handkerchief floating in the water. A bold white stripe between the eyes breaks up the two sides of its head and mantle. These then look like they are not part of the same animal as the white web but instead belong to the darker background. Nothing shows the tasty octopus to the predator, which sees just a white banner billowing against an uninteresting background. As soon as the pounce is completed and the prey ensnared, the octopus stops moving. Then the octopus quickly changes colors to match the sea bottom. The stark white target vanishes from the predator's view.

As they move in broad daylight across the reef, day octopuses change their appearance repeatedly. When still, they match a nearby object. In motion, they become as visible as possible, join a nearby school, and blend in with the swimming fish. A day octopus in slightly murky water will pull all her arms beneath her, assuming a humped shape like a worn coral head or a rock. Using this disguise, she creeps cautiously across the open seafloor. She appears not to move but slowly covers the open distance.

The algae octopus (*Abdopus aculeatus*) holds its arms up to look like a tangle of algae, while it walks briskly on two legs across open ground. The mimic octopus (*Thaumoctopus mimicus*) can look like a flatfish by holding its arms curled backward in a plane against its flattened mantle; with arms held at jutting angles to the sides and banded black, it can look like a lionfish. Both of these fishes have poisoned spines that discourage predators.

Each octopus has many choices to make from moment to moment. When moving across the reef flats, the day octopus changes on average three times per minute. Overall, octopuses can choose from more than a dozen different appearances while out of their dens.

Predators have to know what they're looking for when searching for meals in a busy world. If the prey doesn't match what the predator has in mind, the chance to eat it can be missed. Even three choices for disguise can cut the number of detections in half. This is why simple disguises work, if not perfectly, at least most of the time. Changing disguises a few times per minute, octopuses avoid being seen, recognized, and tracked, even while moving about in broad daylight.

Octopuses live in hostile seas, full of watching predatory eyes in daylight and listening, sniffing, and feeling predators at night. Whether an octopus is out of view, in plain sight, or in disguise, sometimes hiding fails, and a predator finds its prey. Even then, octopuses are formidable opponents.

11

ESCAPiNG OCTOPuSES

Underwater off the Big Island, Hawaii

"COME. COME."

The dive master signaled from thirty feet away in the clear, warm water. I glanced down, where a small, charming day octopus was watching me, motionless. The dive master's sign language grew more exaggerated.

"Come!"

He wanted me closer to the group that, along with my dive buddy, was another fifty feet beyond him. At my slight movement, the octopus retreated. I was making her nervous, and I was making the dive master nervous. As I headed toward him, the dive master turned. When I caught up to him, he had a squirming octopus in his hands.

This one was battered: only three arms remained intact. The rest existed as stumps partially healed and beginning to regrow, or as scars and shreds notched where arms belonged.

The life of this day octopus was one of constant danger. When she failed to escape notice, the soft-bodied octopus was vulnerable. Given half a chance, she used an impressive range of feints, deception, and sacrifices to try to escape with her life. Her successes in escaping by the narrowest of margins were written on her body. I saw this also with many other octopuses: scars and missing limbs or parts of limbs are common.

Her first lines of defense—hiding and camouflage—had at times failed this little octopus. I imagined in those moments she used displays so drastic and terrifying that her disconcerted predator hesitated, winning her the chance to flee.

When seen and threatened, the octopus attempted to scare her attacker. Her arms—before she lost them—curled outward, webbing spread wide and flat, the visible edges of her suckers black. The octopus transformed her entire body into the face of some stark terror. She "painted" eyes on her color-changing skin that were three times the width of an actual eye and covered her entire head. Her white-and-black face was a menacing trick, seeming ready to engulf her would-be predator. The attacker saw in that moment the error it made—and the risk that awaited! Its small target was revealed to be the head of a previously unsuspected giant. In this blink of the predator's second glance, the octopus changed again. Pushed into action, she left an ink cloud behind to hang just where she used to be and jetted away.

Most shallow-water octopus species can produce ink, because it is useful in a sunlit visual environment. Deep-sea species of octopuses often have no ink sac, living as they do in dark habitats where dark ink cannot be seen.

Octopus ink is made of melanin and mucus. Melanin is the pigment that makes the ink dark. The ink gland secretes the melanin-rich black ink into the sac where it is stored until it is needed. This dark ink is long-lasting when used in writing and art. In fact, cephalopod ink gave name to the color sepia (the word originating from the Latin word *sepia*, meaning "cuttlefish").

The funnel organ, attached to the siphon, makes the mucus that the octopus adds to the melanin ink as it is ejected from the sac. Together, the two parts, separately secreted and mixed in the moment, allow the octopus to squirt ink of different forms. With less mucus, the ink she ejects looks like a diffuse smoke screen. With more mucus, the ink holds together in the water as a cloud, called a pseudomorph. This cloud is about the same size as the fleeing octopus. It is likely that octopuses have a sense of how they deploy their ink, although we do not yet know this with certainty.

Let's return to the possible history of the battered day octopus. As the ink blob hung in the water, her attacker was certainly confused. If it persisted in the attack, the predator's jaws would have closed around an insubstantial ink cloud where it expected a bite of octopus. The octopus was already far away, and she had again stopped, camouflaged, and made herself invisible against her surroundings.

Baby turtles will pursue an octopus, and when it inks and jets, the turtles will attack one of the ink clouds. However, having once snapped on an octopus ink blob, that turtle will not again attack an octopus and risk biting into its ink cloud. Ink, it seems, tastes bad to some predators. However, while octopus ink is disliked by the turtles, the smell attracts some moray eels. The inks of different species appear to have different flavors to different predators, including to humans. People find the ink of a squid to be harsh and pungent. But the mellow, velvety-tasting ink of the cuttlefish is palatable to people. In fact, cuttlefish ink is used in Venetian black-dish cuisine.

As for the little three-armed day octopus, perhaps a moray eel came upon her unexpectedly. Or perhaps she was jetting away from one threat only to land on another.

Something like this must have happened to the little octopus in the months before the dive master and I found her, something similar to an attack recorded by snorkelers in Hanauma Bay along the coast of Oʻahu. This time, a moray struck, surprising the little day octopus. She blanched again around false eyes that made her look scary, and at the same moment she jetted away. The moray aimed for the octopus's fake eyes, but its jaws clamped high up on one muscular octopus arm instead. Caught and unable to flee, the octopus engulfed the head and jaws of the eel with her other arms and her web. As the moray twisted, another arm caught its tail. The snorkeler's video showed the small octopus and the larger moray wrestling.

The octopus was ghostly white with black blotches over her head and mantle. While the moray had her arm clamped in its sharp-toothed mouth, the octopus held the moray's mouth closed so it couldn't take any other bites. Her arms were tense and tight, every sucker and muscle engaged in the headlock. Suckers of another arm latched onto the tail, and that arm gradually encircled the body of the eel, holding its tail tight to its head.

The moray felt a suffocating octopus arm reaching inside its gills through the gill slit. Octopus suckers and flesh covered its eyes and nostrils. The octopus held the eel's tail, and so the moray was unable to swim. It thrashed.

But the moray was as agile as the octopus. In two or three twists of its tail, the moray detached the clinging octopus arm, which released reluctantly, almost sucker by sucker. With its tail free, the moray tried one of its best tricks. It curled its tail up over its body, and then around the far side and under again, and finally back through the curled loop above its body. A knot!

The overhand knot is a simple one, but morays can tie themselves into at least five different types of knots, including two types previously not found in the most comprehensive knot-tying manuals.

The moray could then slide the knot forward against the octopus and apply pressure to tear flesh. Although it could not open its jaws or clear its gills with the octopus clamped on and in its mouth, the moray slid its body through its own knot, moving the knot toward its head. The moray slipped this knot over its head with a sudden jerk. In doing so, it entirely tore off the octopus arm clamped in the moray's mouth. The jerk of the knot clearing the moray's head shoved away the rest of the octopus. Finally free of the suckered menace clamped over its head, the moray lurched forward, straightening out its long body.

The very moment she was free, the octopus jetted up into the water, a trail of ink clouds spinning out in her turbulent wake. The moray turned at just this moment and bit into the second ink cloud, but the octopus was no longer there. The entire battle lasted less than thirty seconds.

The eel regrouped, looking exhausted by the fight. Its sole prize, a portion of one arm torn off the damaged octopus, and partly in the eel's open mouth, still clung by suckers over its nostrils and its eyes, blocking scent and vision. The little octopus, although damaged, had escaped.

Long-armed octopuses of the genus *Abdopus*, which includes the algae octopus, can detach an arm much as a lizard can detach its tail. The day octopus lacked this ability, but the sacrificed portion of her arm still clung to the eel's face, helping her to get away. A hungry predator with an arm to eat is less likely to chase a fleeing octopus.

Losing an arm is not as serious an injury as it may sound. Octopuses tighten muscles directly around an injury or amputation, pinching blood vessels and closing them off to stop any bleeding. Given time and good habitat, the octopus can regrow a lost arm.

The loss of an arm or arm tip is a constant risk given the exploratory lifestyle of the bottom-dwelling octopuses. Arm damage is common in wild populations.

Threats to octopus arms are so prevalent that the arms are sensitive to light. When the octopus's eyes are in darkness but a bright light falls on the ends of its arms, the octopus will move the arm tips out of the light and into a dimmer area. This happens even when the octopus cannot see her own arm tips in the light. She pulls them close, where they are less visible to hungry predators. This concern is even more pressing for male octopuses, whose mating success depends on an intact third right arm, which is specifically adapted to pass sperm to the female during reproduction. Even when out actively foraging or exploring, males curl their third right arms in close to their bodies, a behavior not seen in females.

A persistent predator may try to get at an octopus even in a den. Octopuses can block the den entrance to prevent this, sometimes by simply facing their suckers outward, forming a menacing wall. Depending on what is available nearby, the octopus may pull small stones around the den, hold a flat shell across the entrance as a barrier, or use other objects such as a marine sponge or even a discarded bottle as a barrier.

The coconut octopus (*Amphioctopus marginatus*) carries this defense a few steps further. These small octopuses live in open habitats with almost no cover. They make their dens in a clamshell or half of a coconut shell. Finding both halves of the clam or the coconut shell is better still. When available, the octopus will sit in one half and pull the other half overhead, closing the door on its den. Good shelters are rare, though, and the world is dangerous, so a coconut octopus with a good den will tuck both halves under its arms and carry the bulky shelter along while walking across the seafloor on just two legs. If the octopus is menaced, the portable shelter can immediately provide protection.

Octopuses make another defensive use of shells, as seen in the 2020 Netflix film *My Octopus Teacher*. When pursued by a scent-tracking shark, the filmmaker's octopus teacher tried and failed to escape using camouflage and inking. With no den nearby for protection, she made another attempt to fool the predator. She picked up dozens of shells and stones and held one in every sucker, then wrapped her arms overhead with suckers out, becoming an armored ball on the open seafloor.

This did not fool the scent-tracking shark, however. The shark grabbed her and thrashed the ball of octopus and shells. The octopus had to abandon her suit of armor to flee, but she was not yet done with the shark. Moments later, the octopus had somehow hitched a ride on the shark's back, still holding a few shells while comfortably riding along behind the shark's head as it swam. The shark could see no octopus, and any octopus smell was somehow always behind the seeking predator. When the shark passed close by some kelp and rock, the octopus quietly departed, dropping her remaining shells. The shark was none the wiser, despite being schooled by the octopus teacher.

High-stakes predator encounters are not rare for octopuses, which are masters not only of disguise but also of misdirection, fakes and bluffs, and eventual escape. Not every octopus succeeds, but each successful maneuver buys the octopus more time before the next dangerous moment arrives.

PART III
REACH

SENSATION AND THE GRASP OF OCTOPUSES

12

SEEiNG OCTOPUSES

Underwater, South of Sydney, Australia

IT IS A MIDDAY BREAK SIXTY FEET DOWN ON THE SEABED. THE morning rush is over. A gloomy octopus (*Octopus tetricus*) sits with his eyes just above the rim of his den.

Without clear cause, a resting scallop startles and jets itself up. The octopus turns his head with interest at the motion. One Banjo Shark swims into the scene to rest near another. The scallop twists downward through the water to rest again at the bottom. The octopus stretches from its den toward the resting scallop and after a moment reaches two front arms to either side of the prey like a pincer and curls one around the shell.

Both the scallop and the octopus are mollusks. Both see and taste, and both swim by jet propulsion. However, the scallop's vision and swimming method limit what it can do. The scallop may not see precisely where to go, and for many species of scallops, their irregular swimming cannot accurately direct them. In contrast, the octopus has seen and caught his lunch.

Using one arm, the octopus tucks his lunch under his web. Seeking the security of his den, the octopus makes a small jet back to home and at this point drops the scallop.

Why catch the scallop but not eat it? Because once the scallop was out of sight beneath the web, something changed. This was not the first round for this octopus and this scallop. About an hour earlier, the octopus had been out foraging and captured the scallop. He brought it back to the den, dropped it, and seemingly forgot about it. The scallop sat for five minutes where it had been dropped. Then, up swam the scallop, and the octopus reached out toward it. The scallop landed just out of the octopus's sight and was again ignored.

This interaction with the scallop highlights the ways that sight, reach, and touch all interact as an octopus encounters its world.

The eyes of octopuses are large and widely spaced on top of their heads. Their dog bone–shaped black pupils are set horizontally across the white irises. They look out to each side. Like octopus skin, the color of the iris can change from white to golden yellow or darker shades. Each eye sits in a large, round mass of muscle at the top of the head. In a more attentive posture, the eyes either raise up slightly along with the head or pull down a bit. The raised eyes are expressive, like human eyebrows or the ears of a puppy.

Octopuses often move at a diagonal instead of going straight ahead or back. This diagonal movement keeps the center part of their side-facing eye, the part with the sharpest vision, pointed toward the direction they are heading. When moving straight forward or back, the landscape ahead would be viewed through the edges of both eyes where vision is less sharp.

There are two additional striking facts about their vision. First, octopuses do not see color. Second, they do see the polarization of light, which we cannot see.

The underwater world where octopuses live mostly lacks the full rainbow of light needed to perceive color. Shorter wavelengths of light have more energy. This means that wavelengths at the blue end of the visible light spectrum penetrate farther into the water than longer wavelengths. Light that we see as red penetrates least. Only in the shallowest seas are all the wavelengths present so that color can be seen. In deeper water, the available light has only wavelengths in the blue spectrum. Beyond that, it is dark.

The light-sensitive cells in octopus retinas contain only a single pigment, which means that octopuses cannot see color even where the full rainbow of light is present. By comparison, dogs have two different color receptors (in the blue and yellow parts of

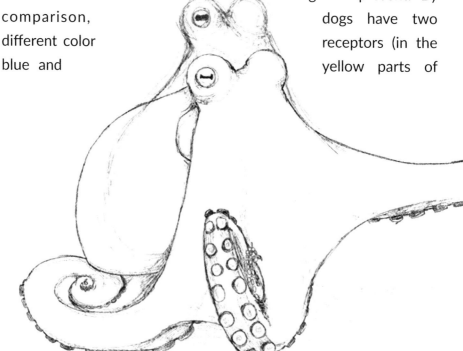

the spectrum). Primates have three (midnight blue, lawn green, and somewhere in the shades of yellow, this last with broad receptivity extending into the red end of the spectrum), and parrots have four (including ultraviolet), which allows their colorful feathers to be even more dazzling to them than the feathered finery is to us.

No known behavior of an octopus demands color vision, although people have tried to find such behavior. Experimenters tried to teach octopuses to differentiate objects based on color alone, but they failed. Octopuses apparently cannot be trained to do this, which itself points to the fact that they do not see color. When octopuses blend in to their surroundings, they match the brightness, shape, and size of their element. All the evidence suggests that most cephalopods lack not only the multiple visual pigment types typically used by animals to distinguish colors but also any ability to use color information to change behaviors.

Despite not seeing color, octopuses *can* see the polarization of light. Our own human eyes do not. Sunlight starts out unpolarized. Unpolarized light is a mixture of waves that vibrate up and down, side to side, and in all the other directions around a circle. Polarized light waves vibrate back and forth in only one flat plane. Light is polarized when it bounces off a flat reflective surface, such as a road, the surface of the water, or the sides of a fish. When you put on polarizing sunglasses, they absorb light waves vibrating horizontally but let the other waves through. This cuts the glare from the road or the glare on the water.

Small particles in water scatter the sunlight as it enters and undo any former polarization. Octopus eyes have photoreceptor cells that tell them how much of the light is vibrating in which directions, in the same way your eyes tell you how much of the light is blue or yellow-orange or green. The polarized light bouncing off the flat surfaces of predators and prey stands out from the background.

Although it did not evade recapture by the gloomy octopus, the scallop attempting to escape can also see. While an octopus has two eyes, a scallop has dozens—up to two hundred, each about the size of the head of a pin, that peer out at the world between the tentacles along the edges of its shell. Scallop eyes have an image-forming mirror and a pair of stacked retinas, features unlike those of any other eyes in the animal kingdom. Scallops, some crustaceans, and the Brownsnout Spookfish are the only animals known to use a mirror instead of a lens to focus an image in the eyes.

What does the scallop do with its mirror and two stacked retinas? The upper of the scallop's two retinas brings the upper part of its visual field into focus and responds to the sight of a distant moving object. It is almost impossible for a diver to approach a scallop without it shutting its shell or swimming away.

The scallop's lower retina focuses on the lower half of the scallop's visual field, perhaps the view of the seafloor from the perspective of a swimming scallop. It may help the scallop find the best living conditions, decide whether to move into brighter or darker areas, or decide when to stop swimming.

Scallops use vision to decide when to feed, opening when they view particles of the right size floating by. They also have the ability to make their pupils smaller in bright light and fully open in the dark, a capability shared with octopuses and humans.

Octopuses have two eyes like people do, but while human eyes face forward—allowing them to work together to create binocular vision—octopus eyes look to either side. The visual ranges of their two eyes don't overlap, so octopuses lack the binocular-based depth perception that we enjoy. The view seen by each eye allows the octopus to create a body pattern to match its surroundings on that same side. The left eye informs body patterns on the left, and the right eye informs the patterns on the right. This means that if one side of the octopus views bright sunlight and the other side views dark shadow, the octopus will turn pale on the bright side and dark, almost black, on the dark side. A sharp border neatly divides the two halves.

With eyes facing to each side, octopuses can see a wide area around them. They do not have to turn their eyes directly toward an object of attention. This makes it hard to know what they are looking at. The eyes can also move a bit forward and back. Beyond these general facts, however, there is little more known about the field of view of octopuses.

How does an octopus know how far away an object is, given their near lack of binocular depth perception? One possibility is that the octopus may get a sense of distance as an approaching object becomes more sharply polarized as it gets nearer. This is much like humans, for example, getting a better sense of the distance of a ship as it approaches through the fog. Another possibility is the use of head bobbing—the vertical raising and lowering of the octopus's head. There is little to no data about when octopuses do this and why. Still, the expectation among those who work with octopuses is that this helps them get a sense of the distance to the objects they see.

Let's return to the example that opened this chapter and add some details. When the scallop first swam up into the water, the octopus turned his right eye toward the swimming prey. As the scallop swam up, and even when it was already far beyond the grasp of the octopus, the octopus still reached out with his first right arm as though to grab the scallop. When this failed, the octopus bobbed his head over a span of about two inches, up and down, once. Twice. Then came a hesitant second reach by the first right arm. But the scallop was too far away. Only then did the octopus begin to move out of his den to approach the scallop as it landed on the seafloor.

Perhaps the first reach failed because the octopus lacked the depth perception necessary to judge how far away the swimming scallop was. The two head bobs gave him more information about distance. The failed second reach might have begun in anticipation of the scallop landing nearer. Finally, with the distance estimated, the octopus made a quick trip over to the resting scallop, surrounding it with two arms.

Unlike on land where animals can see farther in the distance, visibility in underwater habitats is limited by structures such as reefs or kelp forests, as well as by particles clouding coastal and temperate waters. This limited visibility means that octopuses must react quickly to changes in their environment—deciding in split seconds whether to flee, where to land, and when to intercept others approaching, which they do with exquisite sensitivity to their surroundings.

13

REACHING OCTOPUSES

ON FIRST MEETING OCTOPUSES, PEOPLE CAN BE HESITANT TO TOUCH them. There is a twinge of revulsive horror on seeing the sinuous arms—wiggling like worms, or worse, slithering like snakes, and slimy. There is no recognizable face. People often wonder just how fast those serpentine arms of ropy muscle could whip out, coil tightly around, and drag someone into the empty, dark depths?

August 1903, off Victoria, British Columbia

Captain S. F. Scott was yachting with friends for pleasure, but he was about to have a bad evening. He had taken a rowboat out alone, a mile from his friends on the yacht, when he was surrounded by a pod of killer whales. One of these struck the rowboat hard enough that Scott was flung into the water. Scott was amused at first and swam back to his overturned rowboat. Then, as he grabbed the keel, he was seized below the knees and jerked downward with such force that he flipped the rowboat back over on top of his head.

"An octopus!" Scott immediately realized. Kicking hard, he momentarily freed himself and gripped the now upright boat. The octopus again grabbed his legs and pulled downward, as Scott desperately clung to his only support. He described the pain from being pulled as "excruciating," but after long moments, the grip lessened slightly. Kicking with heavy boots and twirling to break the octopus's hold, Scott freed himself. But he was badly injured, the skin of his legs torn and bruised black. Sometime later, his yachting friends noticed the motionless rowboat and hurried to find him half dead from his injuries. It took him seven months to recover.

There are many such gripping octopus stories. There was the hundred-pound octopus that a fisherman could not pry loose from a boat it had grabbed and had to be cut off. There was the octopus that held a man underwater for two hours. I heard stories from Sugpiaq, Eyak, and Haida Alaska Natives about octopuses with a touch so delicate that they could pick blueberries one by one and a grasp so strong they could seize a man or a woman and carry them to their octopus homes beneath the sea. A fisherman recounted how a large octopus that was hauled on deck stole a knife from his belt sheath and stabbed him with it before escaping. Something about the way an octopus looks and moves inspires fear about just what an octopus can do. How strong are they? What are their normal movements? How do they put their unusual form to use in their day-to-day lives?

Captain Scott's story raises these same questions. What does the octopus experience when humans and killer whales disturb the waters above its den? The capabilities of octopuses—their eyes, arms, and suckers—are on full display in this tale as the octopus overwhelms her visitor in a moment.

Captain Scott had about eighty-six billion neurons in his brain, more than 95 percent of the total neurons in his entire body. This proportion is typical of vertebrates. Octopuses are different. The largest parts of the octopus brain are the optic lobes, which process vision, among other things. These contain sixty-five million neurons each, or about 25 percent of all neurons in an octopus body. The rest of the brain contains only another 8 percent of the neurons, for a brain total of about one-third an octopus's nervous system. An octopus has in total about as many neurons as a rabbit, but unlike the rabbit, two-thirds of the octopus's processing power is spread throughout the body.

What do octopuses do with so many neurons outside the brain? Consider the simple motion of the arm that wrapped around Captain Scott's legs. The unfurling of the arm is governed within the arm itself, mostly without checking details with the brain. Many neurons outside the brain lie in the arms, within nerve cords running the length of each arm and connected in chains with clusters of nerve cells, called ganglia, at the base of each sucker and each

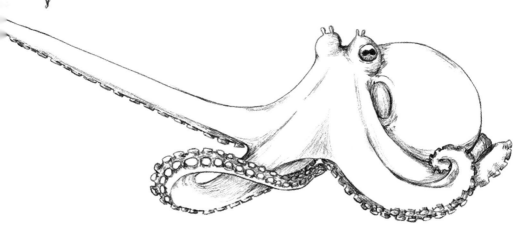

pair of suckers. The arms can achieve much without direct command from the brain, as the coordination occurs entirely within the arm itself.

Familiar animals, including humans, other mammals and all the vertebrates, and the arthropods (insects, crustaceans, spiders), have joints—like your elbows and knees—organized on the principle of levers with paired muscles to move them. But there is no hard skeleton in the octopus's arm. Compared to a human arm, an octopus arm has nearly unlimited freedom of movement. The octopus arm bends, twists, stretches, and contracts and can do so at any point along its length. How is the octopus to decide? To control the motion of a limb that can take a nearly infinite number of shapes, the biology of the octopus must make this problem simpler.

Sometimes, the arm behaves like a whip snapped in just one movement toward an object of interest. When a second arm also reaches, as the gloomy octopus did while catching the scallop for its lunch earlier, the second arm uses the same motion as the first arm.

Lacking real joints, the octopus sometimes makes them where they are needed and discards them when done. To pull an object toward itself, the octopus role-plays a wrist and elbow, dividing the arm into sections similar to the proportions and structure of a primate's arm. The octopus can now bend its "elbow" and twist its "wrist" to do things such as grab a tasty scallop and tuck it to its mouth or pull Captain Scott by the legs below the surface. Then the joints disappear once the task is done. The neurons in the arms provide the control for these motions.

Another way that the octopus accomplishes so much outside the brain is by using the environment to aid its search. Octopuses search by touch along a surface's contours. When a sucker on a surface feels something interesting, it recruits the suckers on either side to also grasp and investigate the object. This process repeats with the next sucker, and so on, until the entire arm has a firm grip on the shape of interest, whatever its contours and whether it is a bit of food, a curious object, or an unfortunate swimmer's legs.

Is the octopus thinking with her arms? The brain does not need to deal with what the arms can do themselves. Holding and pulling an object is just what octopus suckers do to discover what is worth exploring further. The information gathered by the arms goes to the brain, which decides whether or not to let an object go.

Octopuses in motion are graceful. It is also challenging to see how, exactly, they move. The body itself seems not to be involved in the motion, which is accomplished by the arms alone, except when the octopus is jetting. Yet with eight arms all moving at once, and each arm studded with hundreds of suckers also in motion, the force behind an octopus's movement seems invisible.

The resistance of the water limits the speed at which an octopus can move, so that every action appears effortless and made with dignity. An octopus glides along like one driven by gravity or wind alone, but this is illusion, the way a waltzing couple appears to float or a dancer doing the "moonwalk" appears to be stepping forward but is moving backward.

The octopus's eight arms are arrayed in a ring, in numbered pairs one through four, beginning with the pair just below the eyes and ending with the pair beneath the mantle. Octopuses use all eight arms around the body to move in any direction, and they often prefer to crawl at a forty-five-degree angle rather than straight ahead. If the octopus wants to move forward and to the right, it uses its rear left arms to push, and vice versa. Each arm tip stays within its own zone, as octopuses seldom cross their arms when crawling. The direction of movement depends only on which arms are involved in pushing.

With eight arms to choose from, there is no rhythm to an octopus's gait, making it quite different from, for example, a horse's gallop, which has a distinct meter. The complex and mysterious flow of an octopus crossing the ocean floor comes from a series of motions. The arms and sucker stalks bend and straighten. Each sucker may grasp, let go of, or hold any surface it contacts. Finally, octopuses flare and retract the thin web of skin between the arms. As it moves, the flow of water against all these bodily surfaces adds motions of billowing and flapping like a ship's sails in the wind.

An octopus will try to cover some objects with its web and arms. This is visible, for example, when two male octopuses fight. The aggressor may grab with one arm, pulling his opponent under the arms and web. Each rears back, spreading the web and arms widely, reaching to surround the other. If successful, the opponent is enveloped. To flee, the loser must escape the grip of suckers and adopt a streamlined pose to jet rapidly away.

We might expect, with eight arms, that an octopus would carry things in some arms and use the others for walking or crawling. However, carrying objects in extended arms would unbalance an octopus, so objects or prey are carried beneath the web, close to the center of mass. Parts of the first arm pairs may still be exploring or crawling, and arm pairs two, three, and four can be involved in crawling, walking, or even jetting forward. With suckers along the entire arm length, octopuses can hold something close to the body and still put the outer reaches of the same arm to other uses.

Octopuses also sometimes gather material they would like to carry. To do so, the material is gathered by the arms and held in a ball under the web. I have most often seen this behavior used after meals to carry remains of the prey away from the den before discarding them. At that moment, an octopus can look like a walking balloon with tiny suckered legs below—more comical than threatening.

14

SENSATIONAL OCTOPUSES

OCTOPUSES LIKE TO HOLD HANDS. ONCE A PERSON GETS PAST ANY nervousness that the octopus means harm, it's endearing.

For an octopus, holding hands with a person involves many suckers, each of which is holding on some of the time but also busy exploring. Unless there is something unpleasant on a hand, the many suckers don't usually let go all at once. Instead, the octopus arm travels up the hand to the wrist, one sucker at a time. Crevices are interesting: what is under the cuff? Soon the leading part of the arm has crawled into your sleeve. The curiosity to explore, like other abilities, seems to be a built-in part of the suckers and arms.

Earlier in my studies, I had gone subsistence foraging out of Chenega with Mike Eleshansky, and I watched him clean a just-captured octopus for his supper. He sliced each arm off the octopus at its base and tossed them one by one into a bucket. The head and mantle he discarded in the water. I was fascinated to see the arms of the octopus, despite their separation from the

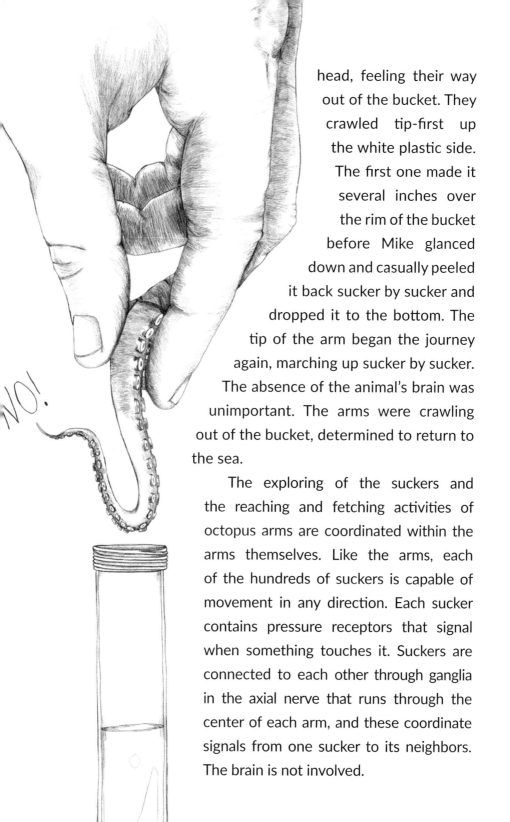

head, feeling their way out of the bucket. They crawled tip-first up the white plastic side. The first one made it several inches over the rim of the bucket before Mike glanced down and casually peeled it back sucker by sucker and dropped it to the bottom. The tip of the arm began the journey again, marching up sucker by sucker. The absence of the animal's brain was unimportant. The arms were crawling out of the bucket, determined to return to the sea.

The exploring of the suckers and the reaching and fetching activities of octopus arms are coordinated within the arms themselves. Like the arms, each of the hundreds of suckers is capable of movement in any direction. Each sucker contains pressure receptors that signal when something touches it. Suckers are connected to each other through ganglia in the axial nerve that runs through the center of each arm, and these coordinate signals from one sucker to its neighbors. The brain is not involved.

For a short time in my career, I collected biopsies from giant Pacific octopuses for an early study on their genetics. Each biopsy was taken as a small, amputated arm tip from a live octopus, and while I disliked having to harm them, partial arm amputation is common among wild octopuses and is a less severe injury than it is for vertebrates. I preserved each biopsy by dropping it into a small vial of pure ethanol. The moment a biopsy encountered the harsh fumes rising off the ethanol, the arm tip would twist and turn away, curling around the opening of the vial as the suckers reached for any alcohol-free surface.

The suckers respond to light, scent, taste, touch, and pain, as well as to their own locations and positions. This gives suckers the information to make their own judgments. When suckers contact something noxious or distasteful, such as the ethanol, the suckers will turn away or will drop it immediately. Occasionally objects that are not interesting but are also not harmful will pass on a conveyor belt of suckers out the length of an outstretched arm to be dropped away from the animal. More often, when an object is interesting or tastes good, it will be passed from one sucker to the next up toward the mouth.

Octopuses can track odors. They have a sense of smell that detects molecules in the water, and as indicated by the ability of an arm tip lowered toward the vial to move away from the fumes, the arms can gather information about the relative location of the odor source. In the dark, without vision, the octopus spreads out to investigate a scent of interest. Then it redirects its path if the extended arms detect that the scent has dropped off as it reaches the edges of the odor plume.

The suckers, despite being out on the octopus arms, also act a bit like the taste buds of humans and some other animals. The sucker rims are packed with touch and touch-taste sensors. Touch depends on receptors that sense pressure and vibration. The touch-taste receptors taste the surfaces they touch and the flavors of molecules that don't dissolve in the water. Touch-taste receptor cells are unique to cephalopods and not found among other animals.

Octopus arms reach into crevices, each exploring arm creeping blindly farther and farther into the space, searching. Possibly the arm will find a tasty crab to capture. But it might find dangers instead, such as stinging anemones, sharp urchins, or abrasive sponges. Touch-tasting suckers that make the first contact can determine whether to hold or release, to advance or retreat—an efficient, fast way to avoid dangers or to catch prey that may flee on touch.

Do the octopus's arms, with their many neurons making local judgments and actions, ever engage in behavior the octopus seems not to intend? How could we know?

Let's return to the story of the gloomy octopus off Australia that twice captured and then dropped his scallop lunch. It was as though the visual system of the octopus recognized the scallop as a desirable meal, so he picked up the scallop and took it back to the den to eat. Once tucked under his web, the scallop was no longer in view. Now the touch-taste system found the scallop unpleasant or uninteresting—and the octopus let it go. Not once but twice. How could this be? Did the gloomy octopus know what his arms and suckers were doing?

This incident might be more understandable after considering the way octopus nerves and brain are built to work together and with knowledge of one more tactic the scallop has to fool an octopus.

Many scallops have a shell encrusted with sponges that often completely cover at least one side of the bivalve. The sponges make it harder for a scallop to swim. So why do the sponge and the scallop team up in this way?

The sponge benefits when the scallop swims. This movement can shed predators, such as sponge-rasping dorid sea slugs. The scallop also benefits by hosting the sponge. The sponge helps to protect scallops from attacks by sea stars, octopuses, and other predators. Octopuses like scallops: they look like food, and their swimming behavior draws the eye. However, octopuses are more likely to eat a bare-shelled scallop than one with a sponge encrusted on its shell.

Once the gloomy octopus had captured the swimming scallop, the scallop left the indecisive octopus's visual system and passed to the taste-touch system. Here the sucker tasted not scallop but the sponge growing on the shell. Sponge doesn't taste like food to an octopus. The well-adapted suckers then released the scallop, which was free once again to swim past the octopus. The octopus recognized an easy meal when he saw one and caught the scallop with his arms once more!

Given that octopuses often forage with their arms for prey they can't see within crevices, it is not surprising the gloomy octopus prioritized taste-touch over sight in choosing food. Octopuses rely on vision for some aspects of their lives. But for the rest, they spread out, touch, taste, and grasp to encounter the world. Still mysterious are the important ways that the octopus's nervous system spreads throughout the arms, suckers, and skin and how these adaptive ways of functioning interact with the brain. Such questions can and are being studied, and clear answers take time to emerge.

OCTOPUS
COGNITION

KNOWING OCTOPUSES

Anchorage, Alaska

"DENA HAS BECOME FEISTY."

One of the student aquarists stepped into my office to report a change. Dena was usually very shy, almost reluctant to interact with anyone. Now, Dena interfered with aquarium cleaning and squirted the aquarists. Worried about the welfare of my charges, I wondered what was going on. Dena, of course, was an octopus.

I began my octopus studies in the coastal fishing town of Cordova, Alaska. I continued them from my appointment as professor of marine biology at a private university in Anchorage, Alaska. The waters of Prince William Sound were not as accessible from Anchorage, located on the traditional lands of the Dena'ina people, but I was nonetheless able to work with many capable and interested students on the curiosities of octopus behavior.

My students and I had designed and built a thousand-gallon-capacity aquarium facility on campus. The main octopus tank provided space for one giant Pacific octopus as long as the individual wasn't too large. A neighboring tank was limited to our smallest octopuses. I trained interested students as aquarists, and they learned a lot of science by taking care of the octopuses and other animals in the aquariums.

Dena's change in behavior started right after we released Calamity—an octopus in the main aquarium next to Dena's—back into the ocean. Calamity had grown rapidly in our aquariums, and when she got too large for our space, we released her back into the wild.

In our care, Calamity lived up to her name, stealing tools whenever possible, squirting water across the room when her tank was open, and pulling anything she got hold of (including nervous aquarists) as far into her tank as it or they would go. Aquarists were

both amused and exasperated by Calamity. She was fun to work with but would not let anyone finish their job in a hurry.

Dena came into her aquarium only one-tenth the size of Calamity. They grew in size in those adjacent tanks, shared the same water, and had a partial view of each other's space, but they had never touched. At the time we released Calamity, shy and reserved Dena was two-thirds the size of Calamity.

A new octopus arrived, and we put her in Calamity's recently vacated space. Clade was quite small, only a quarter of Calamity's size and less than half the size of Dena. Now, with Calamity gone and Clade in her place, Dena underwent a personality change, from shy to bold, from avoiding interaction with the aquarists to an insistence on interacting at every chance.

The change was abrupt. The only event that might have sparked the shift was the arrival of a new neighbor. Dena could see that now she and not Calamity was the biggest octopus in the neighborhood. Had she been shy to stay out of big Calamity's way? Was she now exerting her own will more as she realized she was the biggest octopus around? What sort of judgments do octopuses have to make and what sort of awareness do they have?

Even seemingly simple animals are active and vibrant with life. Sponges pump water through their stationary bodies. Corals pulse and clench; anemones walk and swim. Worms, crabs, lobsters, sea slugs, and squid variously burrow, creep, crawl, scuttle, walk, swim, and jet through their lives, bustling about their business. The lifestyle of every species is unique in some ways. But every living organism is involved with the business of staying alive. That business has certain universal aspects we all have in common. Every animal must eat and discard waste, must shelter from predators and other dangers, and will dedicate its time and energies to creating and protecting the next generation.

Nearly all animals accomplish this business of life through the actions of muscles coordinated by nervous systems. Animal senses feed information about the outside world into the nervous system, allowing muscular action in the world.

Big Calamity's departure and the arrival of little Clade marked a significant change in Dena's visual world. In the wild, this change might offer opportunity. Dena's feistiness suggested she was exploring her new circumstances, not just reacting mindlessly. The demands of new situations—like the arrival of a new neighbor—mean new alternatives have to be considered.

Adjusting to changing conditions requires some understanding of the world. Sensing size is one part of this, and I already knew that octopuses are good at sizing up their food.

Octopuses can tell the sizes of target squares despite varying distances from animal to target. To do this, the octopus must factor in its own subjective viewpoint: it needs to know how far away the object is from itself. Is the object near and small? Or farther away but larger? Taking into account its own viewpoint as the observer is necessary.

Animals do not normally confuse their own actions or movements with movement in the environment. Their own self is taken into account to build the sensory world in which they act. Yet this sensory world develops without much attention to how that world depends on those actions. We think we take the world as we find it. But consider a group of people who were given a belt-and-compass device to wear. The belt vibrated at the precise point around their waist that was on the magnetic north side of their body. As the wearer turned, the vibrating spot on the belt also moved around to remain always to the north. While wearing this belt, the people walked, biked, and hiked outdoors, experiencing the buzz of "north" in their guts, backs, and hips. However, the buzzing faded from their awareness, the way we don't really feel our clothing after a few moments. These belt-wearers quickly found a new understanding of direction. They were better at knowing distances, and their perception of space was better. They found this new map-sense very direct. It was not something they first had to think about. Instead, the vibrating compass belt gave wearers a new sense of direction that was not one of their familiar senses.

We, and all animals, must know how our own actions alter the sensory information we are collecting. Although not always aware of it, such knowledge about their own actions scaffolds the inner lives of animals. We need information not only about the outside world but also about the state of ourselves—our positions, motions, changes, and needs.

New experiences are found while moving, and these make demands of animals. Coping with new situations also requires flexibility in behavior. Some animals have goals in mind and can plan, or they may have learned from repeated experiences. But some behaviors can only change in fixed ways within current conditions. When new situations create uncertainty about the best behavior for success, that is when flexibility matters the most.

Some animal behavior may not be flexible, and an automatic response may be the only one available. Such behaviors have evolved through natural selection to achieve a specific outcome. A classic example is the egg-rolling behavior of the nesting Greylag

Geese. They use their bill to rescue an egg that has accidentally rolled outside the nest. Konrad Lorenz studied animal behavior, and in his research, he removed an egg from under the bird's bill while it was mid-rescue, but the goose continued with the rescue, tucking the egg that was no longer there back into its nest.

Mother digger wasps (in the genus *Sphex*, which means "wasp" in ancient Greek) lack much flexibility at particular moments of caring for their young. The digger wasps excavate burrows and lay eggs in them. They then bring paralyzed insects into the burrow before sealing it up. When the eggs hatch, ample food awaits the newly emerged young. While bringing the food supply for the young, the mother wasp leaves the paralyzed prey at the burrow entrance while it quickly goes inside to check for things that may be amiss. Only after the inspection is complete does the mother bring the prey inside.

A curious experimenter moved the prey a few inches away from the entrance. Mother Sphex, coming out of the burrow, retrieved the prey. As she brought it back, she left it at the mouth of the burrow (again). Bringing prey to the entrance triggered the need for another brief inspection. The experimenter repeated this forty times, and Mother Sphex inspected her burrow forty times, never wavering from routine. This behavioral routine is hard-wired into the wasp. Some wasps never break out of the pattern even after dozens of repeats, while others manage to break the pattern in fewer than ten.

The ability of an animal to respond to new conditions with a new response can help animals succeed. According to one study, terrestrial organisms are more intelligent on average than marine animals because land creatures must consider more possibilities. Air is clearer than water, and so in many environments dangers or opportunities come into view at a greater distance. This allows an organism to consider a larger choice of actions. This opportunity to choose from a number of options—to plan a response—favors intelligence. New experiences demand more flexibility.

To understand the inner lives of octopuses, we must remember how their bodies, nervous systems, and multiple senses interact with the environment as they learn what things look, feel, taste, and smell like. The octopus mentioned earlier that opened the giant butter clam not only got a meal, but also got a lesson about a difficult part of her world and her own ability to pull, to drill, and to bite through shells. Sometimes when a new octopus arrives in an aquarium, the animal is used to eating small crabs. If instead it is fed small, live clams, the octopus, having no experience with clams, ignores them as food. The suckers don't recognize this kind of shell as an item with a meal inside.

But if the shell of the first clam or two is cracked before being put into the enclosure, the suckers taste the potential food when they touch the shell and pick it up. The octopus quickly learns that the shell contains a meal. The octopus begins to laboriously drill open these shells, may try further chipping them, and then after a few meals realizes it is strong enough to pull them open. The octopus accepts clams after that for its meals.

Living in the novel habitat of the aquarium, the octopus combines information from its new environment across its senses and actions, from taste to pulling with the arms to the visual stimulus of the aquarist arriving for mealtime to open the tank.

Animal minds do not always make up a single, well-integrated self. Dolphins and whales sleep literally with one eye open, and only half of their brain sleeps at a time. Pigeons that learn only on one side of the body do not transfer the learning to the other side: their right eye does not know what their left eye is seeing. In some ways, octopuses seem more unified than this. What they learn with one side of the body is sometimes used on the other side. And sleep seems to happen on both sides of the octopus's brain at once.

Still, an octopus's central brain seems not always to have all the information that is available to its arms. Octopuses can determine the shapes of objects they see but not of objects they have only touched. They cannot tell the weight of an object by the drag on their arms. Although there are many sensory nerves localized in the arms, there are fewer nerve channels running from the arms up to the brain. The detailed information the arms can sense is not always returned to the brain but instead can be acted on locally. Octopus arms that have been severed from their bodies, when electrically stimulated, can perform whole-arm actions without a connection to a brain. These include reaching, attaching and releasing suckers, and passing desirable objects mouthward—even though no mouth is actually there. So just how much does the central brain control the arms, and how much behavior is decided down in the arms themselves?

Perhaps the arms could learn without the brain. Perhaps the octopus arms have their own center of awareness. The strongly centralized nervous system organization that vertebrates have—one brain, one mind—stands in stark contrast to the octopus's widespread nervous system.

The growing idea that each octopus arm has its own center of awareness, however, is called into question in two ways. First, octopuses can and do use their brains to control their arms, for example, by guiding arm movement with visual cues. Suckers also release their tenacious hold on objects more quickly when in contact with the brain than they do when isolated. This suggests there is an important role for top-down control from the brain.

Second, cuttlefish can learn the same self-control that children demonstrate in a "marshmallow test": to delay gratification now for a more preferred reward later. In this test, a tempting treat, such as a marshmallow, is placed in front of a child. An experimenter promises that if the child holds off eating the treat until the experimenter returns, the child can have two treats, not just one. Psychologists suspect the ability to delay immediate rewards to reach a larger goal has important positive outcomes later in life.

It should not be surprising that animals, including cuttlefish, can also delay gratification. Although the experiment has yet to be done with octopuses, it's possible that they have the same ability. Imagine that a hunting octopus gets a chance to catch a less-preferred prey. Should it spend time on this one or wait for a better meal to show up? If the octopus expects it can catch something better before returning to its den, then it should not waste time with the lower-quality item. The higher the odds of greater reward in the future, the more it should pass up the inferior opportunity in front of it. The remains of larger crabs found in octopus middens show how much they like bigger prey and suggest that octopuses do just this.

Dena, too, may have been practicing self-control as she watched life in the aquariums and learned and grew. What's more, I suspect the gloomy octopus in Australia could learn to hold onto the swimming scallop that feels and tastes like a sponge long enough to open it and taste the sweet flesh inside.

Dena, meanwhile, has grown larger, which has created new opportunities for her to explore. She is showing many signs of self-knowledge, including learning her own positions and movement, watching her arms, and quite possibly estimating her size relative to others and practicing self-control.

16

DREAMING OCTOPUSES

Anchorage, Alaska

MY LIVING ROOM IS QUIET EXCEPT FOR THE HUM OF THE AQUARIUM pump and gurgle of circulating water. Heidi, our octopus housemate, is comfortable in her home and napping, asleep on the vertical aquarium wall. She displays a mottled mixture of browns splotched with cream. Her mantle tip is dark but lightens toward her head. Below her eyes, she is still paler. The skin over her mantle and head is scattered with small papillae. It's a relaxed camouflage body pattern, but this one is changing, as though she were moving through bands of shadow and light.

Heidi becomes dramatically darker, with ominous stripes flashing on either side. Then she pales. The papillae vanish. A yellow wash blooms, fades, returns, and holds. Then in a moment, her color blackens and her skin wrinkles. Pale again, then a wine color so dark it is black, followed by a deep camouflaging pattern scattered with dark clouds. A curled arm tip twitches.

Heidi is asleep. Why do her body patterns change?

Perhaps she is dreaming. Can we know what an octopus is dreaming?

You sleep every day. You are inactive; you lie down typically. You might roll over, but usually you are not walking around. You can wake up from sleep, but often you simply sleep through things that would get your attention if you were awake. If you don't get your sleep, you will be sleepy the next day and may have an urge to take a nap or go to bed early.

All animals sleep: at least, we have yet to discover cases of an animal that has no cycle of sleeplike behavior. But what is sleep? The actions just noted show how we recognize sleep in other animals. Sleep is not identical to resting. Being less responsive during sleep is different from simply "resting your eyes" or otherwise not moving. You can be woken from sleep, which is different from other forms of unconsciousness, such as being knocked out or in a coma. Sleep is also regulated. You cannot skip sleep without paying the price, and you cannot skip it entirely for long. A certain amount of sleep is required for you to function.

Every species has a typical body position for sleeping, although these are not all the same. Sperm whales, for example, sleep suspended vertically, head up below the water surface, tail toward the deep, and rising at intervals to breathe. Parrotfish sleep while sheltered in a cocoon of their own mucus.

All animals likely have two phases of sleep. Consider the two stages of human sleep. First, as we fall asleep, we enter a transitional state between relaxation and sleep. This lasts just a few minutes as we relax. We then settle into light sleep and eventually reach deep sleep, with very relaxed muscles. Body temperature drops. Our breathing and heart rate are at their lowest levels, and our eyes are not moving under their lids.

At the next stage, while our big muscles remain deeply relaxed, muscles in the eyes, face, fingers, and toes twitch more. In particular, our eyes move rapidly, as though looking at something. Our heart rate increases but body temperature does not. This stage is called rapid eye movement (REM) sleep. The twitching and eye movements make it a high-activity sleep. The early stages of falling asleep, light sleep, and deep sleep are collectively non-REM, low-activity phases. We spend up to 80 percent of our time asleep in the low-activity, non-REM phases and the rest in high-activity, REM sleep. We alternate between the two throughout the night.

Low- and high-activity sleep stages also occur in other animals, probably all other animals.

That octopuses sleep has long seemed the case. Recently, studies of sleep among cephalopods are rapidly increasing what we know. Researchers, inspired partly by the changing

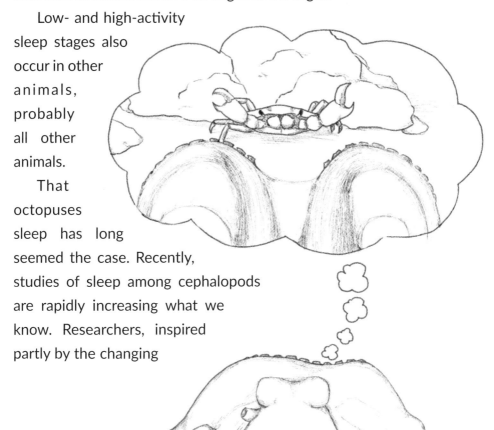

body-pattern activity we observed in sleeping Heidi, filmed medium-sized *Octopus insularis*—a species common in coastal Brazil and its oceanic islands—to learn more about octopus sleep. Often these animals were active or were alert but not active. Sometimes they were quiet but with the pupils still open—not clearly alert but not asleep, just resting.

The appearance of these octopuses was different when asleep. The pupils were closed. Skin color was pale. The researchers called this quiet sleep, a low-activity sleep phase. Short bouts of active sleep interrupted quiet sleep. The periods of active sleep lasted less than a minute each compared to quiet sleep bouts that averaged almost seven minutes. During active sleep, the octopus displayed changing patterns of skin color and texture, as well as rapid eye movements just as people exhibit during REM sleep.

This was how Heidi was displaying when asleep: stationary and mostly relaxed, pupils closed, but arm tips twitching and body patterns changing color and texture. She was asleep, in the active sleep phase. Animal active sleep is not identical to human REM sleep, but there are parallels and similarities.

Often when awakened from sleep, we can recount a dream experience we were having. This happens about half of the time when we awaken from non-REM sleep, and about 80 percent of the time when we awaken from REM sleep. Dreaming is a common human experience, and it's more common during REM sleep than non-REM sleep.

Do animals dream? And if so, can we know anything about it? Or does all knowledge of animal dreams have to wait until, like Doctor Dolittle, we can talk to the animals? Understanding whether animals dream is important for at least two reasons. First, if animals dream, that says something about their consciousness. Second, dreaming is imaginative. In a dream, the experiences of the dream are not actually present; they are assembled—imagined—based on memories and experiences. An animal that dreams is one that can imagine, which is an ability that underlies planning and creativity.

A dream is a mental experience that occurs to the dreamer during sleep. Only the dreamer experiences what is happening in the dream. Most of what we know about human dreaming comes from people telling others about their dreams. But dream researchers use other tools to study dreams as well.

There are at least three ways we learn about human dreaming apart from the actual telling of the dream. We act out some dreams in our sleep. Our brain activity changes. And dreaming helps us learn.

First, normal sleep shuts down large-muscle movements. But sometimes this fails, allowing people to sleepwalk or do other behaviors while still asleep. In this state, sleeping dreamers may act out their dreams. Those who talk in their sleep, if awoken, often describe a dream related to what they were saying.

So these sleep behaviors sometimes reflect dream experience, a fact that still holds even when the dreamer cannot tell about the dream once they're awake. Dreams often are hard to recall, in part because dream experience and dream recall can be independent of each other. Patients with REM sleep behavior disorder have increased muscle activity that allows dreams to be acted out, but these patients do not remember their dreams on waking. It is reasonable to conclude these patients were still experiencing the dream that they were acting out during sleep, even though they didn't remember the dream.

The second way to learn about dreams without telling them is to look at brain activity. Scientists can measure patterns of activity in specific areas of the brain that accompany dreaming. Dreaming stops in patients with damage to one of these areas, a sure sign of their importance to dreaming. Activity in other areas of the brain also hint at dream content. When dreaming of faces, for example, activity occurs in a place called the fusiform face area of the brain. In principle, detailed scanning of brain activity could reveal when a dream is being experienced, something about its content, and whether it might be recalled on awakening. This level of knowledge from brain scanning is difficult to achieve in practice.

Our brains reactivate recent memories during sleep, a process called replay. As the original experience is happening, a particular pattern of neural activity occurs in the brain, forming a new memory. During sleep, the brain replays those same neural patterns at the same pace as the original experience. People who are learning new physical skills and who also sleepwalk have partially reenacted the new skill while sleepwalking. We also replay our new experiences in dreams. Replay is all three of these: neural patterns, sleep behavior, and dreamed experiences.

The third way to learn about dreams without recounting them arises from the effects on learning about the replay of neural patterns in sleep. Zebra Finches aren't born knowing their songs. The finches must learn their songs from other Zebra Finches. To do this, they rehearse aloud, improving their imitation as they practice. The same patterns that fire in the birdsong system of the brain while the finches are rehearsing aloud, researchers discovered, also replay at the same tempo in the brain while the birds are asleep. The sleeping finches further moved their vocal cords as they had during song production but silently. Finally, the "hearing" center of the brain responded as though listening to the soundless neural pattern. The birds were silently rehearsing in their sleep, brains firing, muscles moving, and also "hearing" the same patterns that produce song when awake.

What of Heidi asleep in my living room, arm tips twitching and body-pattern displays moving across her body in waves and sudden starts? We are not certain whether she was dreaming and, if so, of what. But is this something we could figure out? She cannot tell us about her dreams with words. And gathering brain activity information from octopuses in salt water is difficult.

Body-pattern changes are a form of sleep behavior, however. Much like humans talking in their sleep or birds sleep-singing, body-pattern changes are controlled by small muscles, such as those controlling our own faces, fingers, and toes that twitch in REM sleep. Teaching Heidi a new behavior associated with a body-pattern change might lead her to replay that pattern in her sleep, revealing dream content. But already, her body pattern may be enacting her dream.

Octopus displays while battling a predator are different from those seen when pursuing prey or finding a mate or exploring the reef. An octopus attacking prey may move from camouflage to passing cloud to blanched web (but not the mantle) to camouflage again. The detailed sequences of these waking patterns are not well studied. Heidi was not able to tell me about her dream, but possibly she was able to show me.

The expectation that we might learn about Heidi's dreams is uncertain. The pieces are not all in place yet. Just as hearing about a dream is not the same as dreaming the dream, the experience of an animal's dream will always be subjective. Still, behaviors and brain activity that accompany dreams could allow us a little insight into the world of animal dreams. New studies could soon reveal both octopus nightmares and octopus dreams.

PART IV
REVELATION

SOLITARY OCTOPUSES

17

OCTOPUS HUNGRY AND AFRAID

Underwater near Gibbon Anchorage, Prince William Sound, Alaska

THE OCTOPUS WAS OUT ON A FLAT ROCK SHELF AMONG CLUMPS OF turf algae when a dark form emerged into view through cloudy water. The octopus crouched down, spiky, mottled, low, and inconspicuous.

I was the approaching dark shape, and I saw the slight shift that revealed the camouflaged animal. She watched me to see if I was a threat. Her eyes were low out of caution. Her body was flat with arms and web tucked in—except in front. She had a captured meal held under her web and was headed home. Hunger drove her out from her den's safe haven to find food, and fear halted her progress back.

Our emotions—how we feel—determine what we do. Do octopuses really experience emotions? And how do we know? It is not enough to draw a parallel with ourselves. Other animals do have much in common with humans but not always in straightforward ways.

All creatures, including humans, share a deep evolutionary

ancestry that leads to many surprising parallels, despite superficial differences. They also share universal ecological needs—the need to eat, to stay safe, and to reproduce—that can lead to similarities in how each organism functions.

Do animals then share some feelings, like hunger and fear? These feelings are evolutionarily ancient. There are perhaps no more basic feelings than the urges to eat and to avoid being eaten. Australian physiologist Derek Denton named these ancient and demanding urges the primordial emotions.

The primordial emotions Denton identified included thirst,

breathlessness (air hunger), food hunger, pain, salt hunger, muscle fatigue, sleepiness, the urge to pass urine, the urge to defecate, and the urge to regulate body temperature. What these have in common is that they maintain the body in a state of wellness. They also become harder and harder to ignore over time, and each commands a specific action to satisfy the particular need.

In the seas, octopuses move water over their gills by inflating and deflating their mantle a bit like a balloon. The gills extract oxygen from the water. When more oxygen is needed, an octopus will draw more water in over the gills by inflating the mantle more and will inflate and deflate the mantle faster, just as when you're short of breath, you breathe more deeply and quickly to catch up.

Octopuses take six to twelve hours to digest a meal, and all octopuses accept an offered meal following thirty-six hours of fasting. After eating, the octopus shows a reduced tendency to attack. This isn't surprising. An animal without a motivation to start and to stop feeding would either starve to death or burst its gut. But octopuses that have fed are still hungry for exploration, still curious and interested in play.

Octopuses also experience pain. When injured on an arm, the algae octopus immediately inks and jets away to escape the source of harm. But these octopuses also hold the injured arm in their beak for several minutes, much as a human might suck an injured finger momentarily after hitting it with a hammer. Octopuses also curl nearby arms around the injury to protect it from bumping against anything. These protective behaviors last at least a day after the injury. Researchers have discovered that applying lidocaine on an injured octopus's arm numbs the pain as it would for a human.

Octopuses also sleep, as all animals do. Octopuses settle down in a favorite spot, typically their den. They curl their arms around themselves, close their eyes (or at least narrow them), and their breathing slows. If deprived of sleep, octopuses have to make it up later, sleeping longer or at a nontypical time of day.

Octopuses—whether short of breath, hungry, sore, or sleepy—are driven to action by primordial emotions responding to internal sensations, as are other animals. These animals do not confuse their own movements with motion in the world nor their own sensations with events of the external world. Their sense of self, however shaped, is important to coping with their world.

Consider the fact that octopuses at times eat other octopuses. I have found remains of one octopus in the den of another, the dead octopus partially consumed. An octopus clearly can choose to grab another octopus or octopus parts. They have no trouble grabbing almost anything, including octopus skin, and their suckers adhere automatically. Because an octopus's arm may act on its own, how does the octopus know its own arms? That is, how do they know not to grab or eat themselves?

The suckers of *detached* octopus arms, removed from any central brain input, curiously do not attach at all to octopus skin, although they will attach to almost anything else. This provides the first clue to where this self-recognition occurs. Something in the skin stops the attachment reflex of the suckers.

The way that octopuses react to a detached arm provides a second clue to this self-recognition. Octopuses grasp the skin of detached arms with their suckers, hold it to their mouths, and treat it as a food item. But when the detached arm is their own, octopuses touch the arm repeatedly, but the suckers seldom attach. They rarely hold their detached arm in the mouth, but if they do so, the arm is grasped with the suckers only at the amputation site (where no skin covers the flesh). Even then, they only hold it with the beak, while their own suckers avoid it. The octopuses do not hold their own detached arm as a food item.

As these observations show, an octopus can recognize its own skin. The octopus must choose to grip octopus skin. When the brain is not actively paying attention, the suckers do not attach to octopus skin, allowing the animal to swim and move freely without tripping over its own arms or attacking them.

Octopuses respond to their primordial emotions in ways that require some sense of self. Along with other active animals, octopuses alter their own sensory input as they move in the world. They must keep track of their own sensory organs. They must choose behaviors that satisfy their inner drives and appetites. They must somehow recognize their own limbs.

Perhaps octopus emotions and sense of self should be obvious to us. But it is one thing to just assume that, clever as octopuses are, they have complex inner lives. It is something else to defend that assumption scientifically. And it is yet another to fully understand it.

Primordial emotions—the first motivations—are major drivers, but they are not enough by themselves to allow the animal to meet its needs through action. In addition, octopuses must be able to sort through the opportunities they find in their environment and decide what to do. Their awareness is shown by the choices they make in the face of opportunities.

18

OCTOPUS CANNIBALS

Bahamas

A COMMON OCTOPUS KEEPS HER EYES HIGH.

She can just see over the coral head, now dead and overgrown with algae. Meanwhile, three and then four arms are reaching under, into, and through the available crevices and holes. Two Bluehead Wrasse swim by. They are not focused on her, and she ignores them.

On the far side of the overgrown coral rock, her reaching arm touches—what? Something small instantly flees. Her attention now on that arm, she pales and pounces to that side of the coral. She can now see the fleeing quarry, and she pushes off from the dead coral, jetting after it. The small, fleeing animal makes a nimble left turn. The pursuer spreads her arms, the one nearest the target whipping out toward it, but she misses.

She turns now, jetting and reaching in a pounce that covers the distance traveled by the small, fleeing form. As she ends her

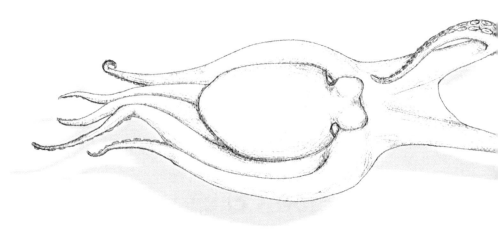

leap, with the quarry at eye level in front of her, her pale, uniform color vanishes, replaced by mottling and a dramatic black edging of suckers along each arm. The prey inks and jets away. It is a smaller octopus, less than a tenth the size of its opponent, and it is using every octopus escape tactic against its larger kin. The ink cloud is small and is left behind in the chase. The tiny, jet-propelled octopus is widening its lead over the larger pursuer. The larger octopus then leaps again after the tiny prey, mottle turning back to a pale color as she leaves the bottom.

She jets up into the water, flinging out the first right arm, and the smaller octopus flees upward. The pursuer's arm, moving almost too fast to intercept the target, brushes along the fleeing octopus, touches small trailing arms, then head, and finally the forward mantle. Somehow, as the two make contact, one small octopus arm is grasped by the suckers of the pursuer. The pursuer now coils her arm, twisting around to grab the prey by a single one of its tiny arms. The pursuer is able to wrap the smaller octopus into two of its large arms and a billow of web, surrounding it. She then falls back onto the reef

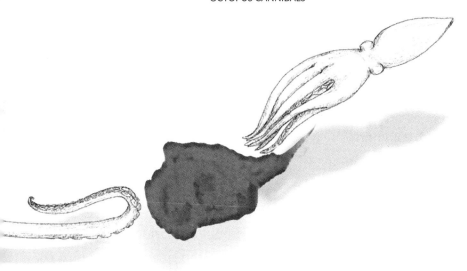

with her prize. When her arms touch the bottom, she changes in a moment from pale coloration again to a camouflaged mix of browns and cream mottles and stripes and settles in to devour her meal.

Octopuses eat one another. No wonder they spend their lives alone.

In the ocean, the food web is often size-based. At the bottom of the food chain are small phytoplankton suspended in the water that are growing from the energy of the sun. Water is about eight hundred times as dense as air, so many particles that would fall to the ground from the air will hang in water. Floating algae (phytoplankton) are fed on by small animals (zooplankton) that are also suspended in the water. Larger zooplankton feed on smaller ones. Small fish feed on the larger zooplankton. Many species hatch out as plankton, even though they will become large as adults and will thus occupy higher levels of the food web as they grow.

Cannibalism is common in the animal kingdom, particularly so among water-dwelling animals. Cannibalism among marine animals is usually size-based, including among the cephalopods. All species of the cephalopods are carnivores, hunting or scavenging their prey. Among squid, cannibalism of smaller individuals by larger has been reported commonly in twenty or more species. Cannibalism also appears common among the most-studied cuttlefish species.

A few individuals of the Maori octopus (*Macroctopus maorum*) captured in a New Zealand study contained octopus eggs of their own species in their guts. When kept together in aquariums, larger Maori octopuses attacked and attempted to eat the smaller ones and also attacked a smaller species, the gloomy octopus, when the two were housed together. Another octopus can represent a large meal: by weight, octopuses make up the largest part of the Maori octopus diet. The guts of 8 percent of wild Maori octopuses contained the remains of their own species. Cannibalism by the Patagonia octopus (*Octopus tehuelchus*) and the southern red octopus (*Enteroctopus megalocyathus*) may be similarly common.

Females can also attack and eat smaller males. In at least a few species, including the wonderpus octopus (*Wunderpus photogenicus*), the day octopus, and the gloomy octopus, the attacking octopus will attempt to strangle another octopus, using its arms in a chokehold across its prey's gills. For this reason, encounters with another octopus always appear to be dangerous affairs, despite being necessary for mating. Smaller males, even while interested in mating, act wary when close to females. There is not always a size difference between males and females in mating octopuses, but larger females are likely to lay more eggs and hence may have higher reproductive value. So males are interested in mating with larger females when they find them, despite the risk. Factors such as male suitability as a mate and female hunger levels, in addition to size differences, may also figure into when octopus cannibalism occurs. Often the individual that becomes prey is half the size or less of the predatory octopus.

Cannibalism by octopuses is one reason they have a reputation as solitary animals. They are usually found alone rather than in groups. In a few situations, however, octopuses interact with others in ways that contradict their solitary reputation. Even animals of other species have been found to share dens with octopuses. And waders, snorkelers, and scuba divers sometimes feel befriended by them. Do octopuses in the wild have a sense of themselves in relation to others? Do octopuses have the ability to form relationships?

19

OCTOPUSES IN WILD RELATIONSHIPS

Underwater, South of Sydney, Australia

THE GLOOMY OCTOPUS SAT IN HER DEN, DUG UNDER THE EDGE OF an overgrown and encrusted lump of metal. From here, she could look out on the passing fish, watch for approaching dangers, and perhaps even see a possible meal moving past. Next to her in the same den were three fish—all Bearded Rock Cod. Rock cod, smooth red fish with orange lips and chin barbels like sensitive fleshy whiskers, seek and feed on small, bottom-dwelling crustaceans. The three fish pressed against each other, or nearly so, facing out of the den alongside the octopus. There was hardly more space between the octopus and the nearest fish than between the fish themselves: in fact, they were touching at times. The four looked very much at home together, like long-familiar roomies.

The octopus actively maintained her den space, excavating it to prevent the cavity from filling in by waves or storms. She may have to defend the space against intruders. The cod, as far as we know, do not contribute in similar ways.

The fish benefit from the shelter the octopus built. But what did they bring to the household? Possibly nothing. Perhaps the fish do not bother the octopus or are too difficult to evict. Having them there may cost the octopus nothing. This may be the case, although the octopus could quite easily make a meal of the closest of these. Why doesn't she? Perhaps the cod help the octopus keep the den free of pests because they feed on such small crustaceans. But the octopus periodically cleans the den herself. The large fish seem to be unlikely, cumbersome predators within the den.

Could the octopus just like the company? Can some invertebrate animals such as octopuses form relationships with other individuals?

Octopuses in aquariums certainly seem to do so. Caretakers soon recognize whether a particular octopus likes or dislikes them, perhaps by its expressive color changes or a habit of shooting jets of water at people they dislike. Octopuses recognize their caretakers, but they also recognize other octopuses, fishes, and predators or prey, and see them as different from other moving objects such as wafting kelp or debris drifting by.

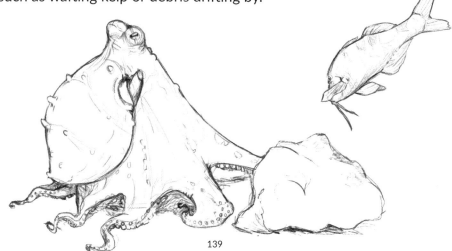

The fishes, the crabs or scallops, and the other octopuses fall into important different categories—some dangerous, some tasty, others neutral or uncertain. Each category may require a specific action. By matching their behavior to the creatures they meet, octopuses are able to thrive in their watery realms. These behaviors show their ability to categorize their environment and the creatures in it. Many octopuses, for example, will engage with a curious diver in ways they do not with an investigating sea lion. When divers tested day octopuses, some reached out to touch a pencil held toward them rather than showing fear. But when investigated by a sea lion, a wise octopus will retreat farther into its shelter.

Animals have evolved to categorize objects and other creatures in their environment that are important for their survival. In humans, specific areas of the brain are dedicated to the categorization of human faces; to animals, fruits, and vegetables; and to useful objects such as scrapers and knives. Evolution shapes the same capabilities in other animals.

This ability in octopuses was made clear to me one day while diving in Jervis Bay, Australia, where the octopus kept house with the Bearded Rock Cod. Parts of this bay lie within Booderee National Park; the Koori people of the Dhurga-speaking Yuin nation are traditional owners of these areas.

Booderee translates as "plenty of fish." This was true on the day of my dive. As part of a dive team, I was setting out cameras mounted on small tripods and weighted to stay on the seafloor. As we neared the bottom, we descended through schools of hundreds of fish, each fish a bit larger than a hand span. We wanted to record octopus behavior. On the shell-strewn ocean floor, we settled the cameras down among the Eastern Fortescues and the Blacksaddle and Bluespotted goatfish that shared the area.

Of particular note on the seafloor was a mound, six feet or more in length, covered with floral, milky spots amid browns and blacks. It was fringed at one end and had the distinctive two dorsal fins and tail of a shark at the other end. This was a large Gulf Wobbegong, whose small eyes hid among its camouflaged body patterns. The shark lay motionless at the edge of our study site. Knowing these animals are lunging predators, we cautiously never swam in front of it as we placed cameras around the site. Then we left, with the cameras recording our data.

We returned hours later with replacement cameras, as the battery life on the first set had run low, and repeated our tasks. I had read that although wobbegongs rarely attack divers, they have sometimes clamped on an arm or leg when a diver foolishly ventured too close. Although their teeth inflicted some damage, these are not the sharp, severing teeth of White or other familiar sharks. The wobbegong, however, holds tight and does not let go, creating a life-threatening situation for such an unfortunate diver. So our team was extremely careful to go above the shark rather than in front of it as we swapped out the cameras and returned to the surface.

I quickly reviewed our video recordings, looking for signs of interesting behavior from octopus dens. But at each den, the octopus stayed out of sight for the entire recording. Only one remarkable moment appeared on the morning video. A school of Greenback Horse Mackerel swam back and forth over the motionless wobbegong, staying well above it as the other divers and I had. Without warning, the wobbegong lunged suddenly *upward* and grabbed an unfortunate mackerel. So fast was the upward lunge and capture that it happened almost between video frames.

I showed my colleagues this exciting moment immediately. On our final dive to retrieve the video cameras, no one dared to swim over the motionless wobbegong again.

More interesting still was how the octopuses behaved. Usually, an octopus will sit in the den's entrance, groom itself, move shells, carry the remains of a meal a few body lengths away to dispose of them, and come and go to forage or do other business. When the wobbegong was nearby, however, all activity stopped. Octopuses did not sit at their entrances, didn't come and go, didn't even make themselves visible.

There was one exception. In the late afternoon, as day faded to twilight, a gloomy octopus cautiously crept into view inside the den opening, emerging between the three Bearded Rock Cod. Fifteen minutes later, the octopus had gradually crept forward and was sitting in the mouth of its den. The wobbegong noticed. It crept closer to the den, as though merely shifting its body in place. It took nine minutes for the shark to move one body length nearer the octopus. Despite its efforts to escape notice, the octopus saw the approach, and its eyes raised high on alert. The wobbegong lifted awkwardly off the bottom to twist directly toward the den, and it landed its head and mouth less than half a meter in front of the den opening. During this motion, the octopus retreated completely into its den and could no longer be seen. Half a minute later, the wobbegong returned to its previous position on the edge of the site. There was no other octopus activity that day and the next while the wobbegong remained there.

This extreme caution around a fast-lunging, sit-and-wait predator seems wise, but it is also a revealing behavior. Octopuses do not react in the same way to every predator. An octopus may freeze briefly or adopt a more camouflaged body pattern when a fast-moving predator looms into view, but once the predator has passed, normal activity returns. Swarming predators, such as the sometimes aggressive Ocean Leatherjackets (one of the Australian fish species hanging around the area) are usually ignored if near the den, despite the fact that they can mob and kill an octopus that finds itself without shelter. On one occasion, we recorded an Ocean Leatherjacket that took a bite out of an active and very visible octopus. The octopus flinched at the wounding, and immediately afterward spent more time in its den than it had previously, but within five or ten minutes resumed normal activity. Only the presence of a particular kind of predator shut down octopuses for the entire day—a sit-and-wait predator such as the wobbegong that lurked motionless nearby, awaiting a careless move.

Octopuses also tailor their behavior to hunt their prey. An octopus does not lunge at a swimming scallop but reaches out almost lazily to grab it. The scallop has limited ability to direct its escape. The same octopus, however, will stalk a fish and pounce in attack. The fish, of course, is good at directing its own escape, particularly if it can see or feel the approach. The octopus is reacting to different categories of predators and prey. One is fast and agile, another is slow and clumsy; one is a passing threat that can soon be ignored, while others must lurk in memory as they lurk nearby, lest a careless moment result in death.

Octopuses are well equipped to recognize and react to these different categories. Octopuses are active and curious. Using flexible arms and suckers, they have a variety of ways of acting on the world, such as pouncing, pulling and pushing, holding and releasing. Their impressive sensory abilities—including recognizing motion, form, and light polarization; the touch-taste of their suckers; and sensitivity to water movements from pressure sensors in the skin—all help them sort their world into the many kinds of opportunities and threats.

When an octopus recognizes which of these it faces, it also identifies the role it will have to play. Sometimes, the octopus is a lethal predator, searching and pouncing or taking other predatory actions. At other times, the octopus itself is stalked, and it hides, inks, or wrestles as dire circumstances demand.

These fundamental roles appear everywhere in the biological world, but octopuses adopt other roles as well, requiring different sets of responses. Another octopus might be possible prey or predator but also could be a potential mate. Some fish may be neither predator to evade nor prey to attack. Octopuses tolerate attention from cleaning gobies, for example, even allowing these slender fish to enter their siphon. The day octopus can also tell when a fish is referring to something—that is, pointing, fish-style.

On my first diving trip to Australia, I was excited to encounter my first day octopus. The water was clear, the octopus was actively exploring the corals, and during the encounter I focused on taking photos. Only afterward, while reviewing the images, did I realize that in every exposure I had also captured her fish friend, a coral trout that was always by the octopus's side.

Coral trout are drawn to foraging octopuses and join their search on the reef, perhaps to catch any small prey that escape the octopus or to pick at shells it drops. The coral trout may also do a headstand over a crevice where some quarry has escaped and is now out of sight of the octopus. It is pointing—to indicate "Here is food I cannot get at." The octopus will then approach the pointing trout and

OCTOPUSES IN WILD RELATIONSHIPS

explore the indicated reef crevices. The coral trout do not make this gesture when no octopus is nearby. In the Red Sea, coral trout and groupers behave the same way, enlisting the help of predators such as moray eels and Humphead Maori Wrasse to uncover prey in tight hiding spaces on coral reefs. The groupers sometimes also draw the attention of these fishes by performing a whole-body shimmy in front of the moray or wrasse they are recruiting.

Coral trout and groupers use these behaviors to alert another animal where prey may be hiding. They are cooperating with each other for greater foraging success.

Pointing of some sort is not widely found among animals, but it does occur in a few species. Apart from humans and their dogs, the great apes, dolphins, and ravens also point to communicate with one another. These are all animals renowned for their social lives. But below the waves, the solitary octopuses and the fishes are pointing across the species barrier, connecting not to family or flock mates but to a found companion, agreeable company for a day of foraging on the reef.

Octopuses pay close attention to the eyes of those watching them. In one diving encounter in Alaska, an octopus clung to the kelp, camouflaged, as we watched each other. I turned my gaze for a brief second to find the collecting bag clipped to my dive belt, but when I glanced back up, she was gone. In another excursion off the island of Mo'orea in French Polynesia, an octopus I had been following hid behind a coral, raising only his eyes above the edge to observe me. On the other side of the rock, the octopus would have been in plain sight. He hid from me by acting on my point of view. Octopuses show their awareness of us, their understanding that we may be important actors in their environment who carry intentions or goals that could matter to them.

These abilities are the foundations that support basic relationships, so we should expect octopuses to have them. Indeed, at one level—the relationships of predator to prey, of prey to predator—they are inevitable. Octopuses carry this further, relating to the intentions, position, and attention of others in complex ways. Despite being solitary animals, octopuses could be in relationships with others. If so, do octopuses ever gather? What happens then?

SOCiETY OCTOPUSES

20

GATHERING OCTOPUSES

Underwater, South of Sydney, Australia

THE OCTOPUSES CERTAINLY SAW ME COMING. I DOVE DOWN ABOUT sixty feet toward a sandy plain interrupted with clumps of algae and scallops. From above the seafloor, I saw a patch that stood out from the sandy plain. It was a pile of thousands of scallop shells. Octopuses, including gloomy octopuses, usually live solitary lives. But here in this shell bed roughly the size of a typical living room, as many as sixteen octopuses can be found living in close quarters. Scallops are their main food, and the emptied shells have piled up around a single, human-made metal object, probably dropped from a boat. The object is about as long as my forearm and is now mostly buried, but octopuses still dig out one or two dens along its edges. The shells of their meals are scattered at the mouth of the den. As these discarded shells pile up, they make it easier for the octopuses to create a place to live.

This is Octopolis. It was discovered some years back by local diver Matt Lawrence. He and his colleagues now visit the site a few times a year to learn more about the octopuses that live here. The area can be very busy in the Australian summer and nearly deserted in the winter. There have been octopuses here over many years. Because gloomy octopuses do not live more than a year or two, the octopuses we find here one season are not the same ones we return to the next.

A small octopus in a den along the edge of the site leaves her shelter. After moving into the nearby algae, she pauses. Her skin is scattered with raised papillae that help her blend in with the algae fronds. Once motionless, she is hard to pick out from the background. After a few moments, she starts traveling again, until she is about ten feet from her den.

The live scallops close by Octopolis are small and sparse because the octopuses have already eaten the bigger ones. If she travels farther out, there are two to three times as many scallops, and they are often twice as large. But the farther she goes, the riskier it is. And while it's not exactly safe in Octopolis, staying close to her den is safer than traveling farther to where the big scallops are found.

She covers a clump of scallops with web and arms, and her body jerks slightly in a tugging motion as she pulls the biggest ones free. Then, carrying the scallops under her web in front, she hurries back to her den in a rapid walk. Once in her den, she sits for twenty minutes eating her meal.

When she is done eating, the small gloomy octopus pushes the cleaned scallop shells left from her meal onto the low mound of discards surrounding the mouth of her den. The cumulative discards of many octopuses over time creates a habitat for the small animals that come to graze the algae that grow on the shells or to prey on the worms and barnacles living in the pile.

This shell bed also draws a surprising diversity of fish. In addition to the Eastern Fortescues and stonefish, a Dwarf Lionfish wedges its spines along an encrusted ridge of the metal object. Banjo Sharks, like mats across the seafloor, often lie atop one another. Port Jackson Sharks with black eye masks sit among them, and a few broad Kapala Stingarees rest here and there. A cow-eyed porcupinefish wears a look of perpetual joyous surprise. Roaming in the water just over the area are brown-striped Ocean Leatherjackets, while hundreds of silver mackerel swim around and over the site in a dense swarm that obscures the view as they pass.

The seabed everywhere around is made of loose silt or sand at least a foot deep with no solid surfaces, covered only in this one spot by discarded scallop shells in a pile that surrounds the metal object. About one kilometer away, however, is another area less than twenty meters across, where bedrock emerges from the sediment. At this second site, too, we found octopuses living along the edges of the rock, where they had also accumulated the shell hash of discarded prey remains. Within meters of this spot, there were rich beds of doughboy scallops and mud arks, another type of bivalve.

The number of octopuses at these two sites suggests that octopuses are drawn to them. The octopuses live within sight of one another and are keenly interested in one another. The abundance of food within a few meters of each site makes these spots desirable. The octopuses do not have to go far from their dens to get each meal.

Because octopuses routinely discard empty shells at the den after the meal, perhaps the mound around a den can get too high over time. We recorded some octopuses carrying the remains away from their dens to the edge of the shell hash and dumping them there. More shell hash means room for more octopuses, and more octopuses amass yet more discarded prey remains.

The loose silt and sand all around are grown over with algae and make good habitat for scallops and mud arks. But silt and sand and mud allow little shelter for these octopuses, which den in reefs and under rocks. Many predators and dangers swim through these waters, so shelter is a requirement for the octopuses. Octopolis appears to have been started because of the presence of the man-made metal object, whatever it is. The second site, however, where bare rock emerges from the silt, and which we nicknamed Octlantis, is entirely natural.

In these waters, where food is abundant, predators common, and suitable shelter rare, an octopus cannot be choosy. These locations that provide good shelter and nearby food choices bring the octopuses into contact with one another. This, as it turns out, forces them to interact. They do not turn to cannibalism, however—which is perhaps surprising.

There are a few other situations where octopuses engage with each other. In the late 1970s and early 1980s, the Larger Pacific Striped Octopus reportedly formed colonies of thirty to forty individuals. It was a striking species, about a hand span in size and one of a few species of harlequin octopuses, distinguished by semipermanent stripes and spots visible among nearly all body patterns. But the account of this animal's behavior was unlike any other octopus. They shared dens in mated pairs, mated beak-to-beak, and laid eggs over extended periods so that some eggs were already hatching as the female was still laying and tending more. How could this be the case in a group of animals known for their cannibalism, cautious and distant mating, and death after tending eggs? A full scientific description of these behaviors was rejected at that time, and the account was never published.

This octopus species disappeared after the early 1980s. It became almost legendary: had the species gone extinct? There the situation rested for almost twenty-five years. No one knew how to find further wild populations or even if they still existed.

Then, in the summer of 2012, a few octopuses matching the description of the Larger Pacific Striped Octopus showed up in the aquarium trade. They had all been collected at one location in Nicaragua. The Steinhart Aquarium in San Francisco acquired many of these octopuses and displayed them to the public for a short while. In 2015, Roy Caldwell and other scientists published a study of their behavior in captivity that matched the earlier observations from the 1970s. Despite ongoing interest from the aquarium scientists, after the discovery in Nicaragua, no more wild Larger Pacific Striped Octopuses could be found for further study.

There is one other octopus species (*Octopus laqueus*), found in Japan, where male and female mated pairs also share a den. They live close together in the wild, and males and females in captivity will tolerate sharing a den if that's their only option, although they would rather have their own den. In short, they balance the need for shelter against the desire to avoid others. They are more tolerant of each other than are many octopuses. It may be the same balance sought by the gloomy octopuses in settling at Octopolis and Octlantis.

The algae octopus is another species involved in common encounters with each other. This is the long-armed octopus that can drop part of its arm when attacked. They are active during the day in intertidal shallows where larger females maintain dens. Males interested in mating occupy dens next to these females, to be within arm's reach—that is, within mating distance. Dens are clumped together, and males on the move encounter other males in their own dens. These males will fight, and the winner is usually the larger of the two. Octopuses on the move also encounter members of the opposite sex, and these meetings can end in mating, or in ignoring one another, or even in cannibalism, where the larger female eats the smaller male. In other words, male algae octopuses seeking to mate face a high risk of aggression from other octopuses.

Monterey Submarine Canyon, off the Central Coast of California
On a canyon wall close to a mile down in the ocean, high currents expose bare rock. Such hard, exposed habitats are rare in the deep sea. On this rock outcrop, a female *Graneledone boreopacifica* octopus tended her eggs for nearly four-and-a-half years. A remotely operated vehicle first filmed her in April 2007 and visited her repeatedly until October 2011. Octopus mothers do not hunt or feed while they are

tending their eggs, and this female was no exception. For more than four years, she ignored nearby prey and refused food offered by the vehicle operators. The female and her developing eggs were still there in September 2011, but she was gone in October, with just the tattered cases of her hatched eggs to mark the spot. Tropical octopuses may brood their eggs for a few months, but in colder water, it takes longer. The giant Pacific octopus, a cold-water species, tends her eggs for about six months. But the colder the water, the longer the brooding time required for the eggs to develop. The deep sea is cold indeed, and this female *Graneledone boreopacifica* octopus holds the record for the longest brooding period known for any animal. In the deep sea, exposed hard surfaces draw egg-tending octopuses or fishes because these rare habitats offer a surface where eggs can be attached. In one such area, researchers counted more than two hundred octopuses, at times close enough to one another that a single photograph captured at least eight of them.

The material or structure of the ocean floor can be very important to octopuses. When shelter, mating opportunities, or brooding sites are scarce or occur in patches, different species of octopuses must tolerate being near each other. In some cases, there may be enough space that brooding octopuses do not interact much with each other. This appears to be the case on the deep-sea canyon walls. However, on nearby Davidson Seamount, nearly three thousand female *Muusoctopus robustus* mothers clustered their nests around spots where warm water seeps out of the rock, each egg-tending octopus within easy reach of neighbors. At Octopolis, in the dangerous waters south of Sydney, octopuses bringing their meals back to a safe den to eat have built up a pile of shells that forms new habitat, and they now must cope with new neighbors nearby.

Neighbors are a challenge if octopuses have evolved to be

solitary, without ways to cope with other octopuses. Mating and cannibalism do not fall into this gap, but what of behaviors in between courting and killing? Can these octopuses relate to each other in any different ways?

Underwater, South of Sydney, Australia

A gloomy octopus pushed at a shell. A moment later, the octopus, a little female, pulled fully into her den hollowed into the scallops and silt. Under her arms, she gathered a load of loose shells and debris that had settled from the sides and edges. She rose up, lifting everything to the lip of the den and sat a moment, checking for dangers. Cautiously, she left her den, carrying the debris a short distance, and then dropped it all. The octopus hurried back to her den. During the next half hour, she repeated the action twice, conducting three den-cleaning trips in all. In her den again, she pushed and arranged a few more shells on the edges.

Were these behaviors automatic reactions to the shells shifting in her den—a response that unfolds without attention or thought? Or was this octopus thinking about how she would like her den, tidying up with a more orderly home in mind?

After tidying, she sat on the edge of her den a while, watching the water around her. Fish swam by frequently, some dangerous, some not. Then she left her den, traveling farther across open ground than she previously had to dump the debris. When she returned to her den, she was carrying a large black sponge she had picked up, about half the size of her mantle. She dropped down into the safety of her den, holding the sponge on the lip of the den. She retreated into the opening and, with her last arm to enter, pulled the sponge after her. The sponge filled the den entrance, forming a door.

The arrangement of objects around her den entrance, the attentive removal of debris, the fetching from a distance a sponge particularly suited to block the opening—these appear to be intentional behaviors.

During the half hour this little octopus was den-cleaning, other octopuses in the area were active as well, close enough that the little female knew of their presence. How might she regard these other octopuses—these predators or mates or, perhaps, neighbors? Certainly, the sponge could serve as a barrier against predators, but was it also a door to close for privacy from socially curious neighbors?

21

OCTOPUS QUIDNUNCS

Underwater, South of Sydney, Australia

ON THE SOUTH EDGE OF OCTOPOLIS, A LARGE, FEMALE GLOOMY octopus rose up out of her den and began to move toward the edge. A male octopus, also large and resting a few body lengths away, noticed the female's movement and reached out a long arm toward her. He began to move in her direction. She pulled back into her den. A few minutes later she tried again; he reached again. She moved out a bit farther, and he approached. She retreated into her den a second time. On the third try, without hesitation, she headed out of her den and directly off-site, toward the sand and algae flats where live scallops abound. He reached again and approached, but this time she ignored him.

Male and female octopuses look similar, although there are some differences. We can more often tell males and females apart in our videos by their behavior. The male octopus mating attempt is distinctive. He reaches for a female with the third right arm and typically covers that arm at the base with the second right arm. Except when attempting to mate, males are careful of their third right arm and carry it curled and tucked protectively a bit closer to the body than the other arm tips. Even when not mating, however, male gloomy octopuses in Octopolis behave quite differently toward females than toward each other.

As another female exited her own den near the center of the shell bed, the same male redirected toward her and trailed her to the edge of the site. He was reluctant to follow farther. Minutes later, an octopus approached from off-site, bearing the rewards of a foraging trip. As she first came into view in the distance, the large male alerted, raising his eyes and turning dark. Then he stood tall on his arms and lifted his mantle. He appeared large and ominous as he approached the arriving female octopus cautiously. He reached toward her, but she skirted to one side around him. The male and female touched or reached just shy of contact. Then the male's caution, his dark skin, and tall posture all collapsed at once. He dropped into a walking stance, his skin lightened, and he went with the female to the recently vacated southern den. She settled there and began her meal. He behaved the same way with the next arrival, which went to the central den carrying a meal of scallops under her web.

The large male seemed to have a particular role. He is the octopus Quidnunc here. He pays attention to every octopus that moves. He is the most active octopus, and it is as though he were asking "What now?" when an octopus moves in the den or "Who is that?" as one returns to the site. Although we often found a Quidnunc in Octopolis over the years, it was not the same male octopus each time because of the short life span of gloomy octopuses.

The Quidnunc seldom occupies a den when there are other octopuses to visit, and he rarely leaves the site. He spends his day crossing and recrossing the shell bed to inspect each octopus that comes or goes or draws his attention. This octopus does not behave like females on the site, and if there are other males about, they do not behave like this male either.

Does the existence of such a role require that octopuses be able to recognize each other as individuals and form relationships? We are still learning whether   octopuses identify each other in this way.

Distinctive marks or scars   allow people to recognize

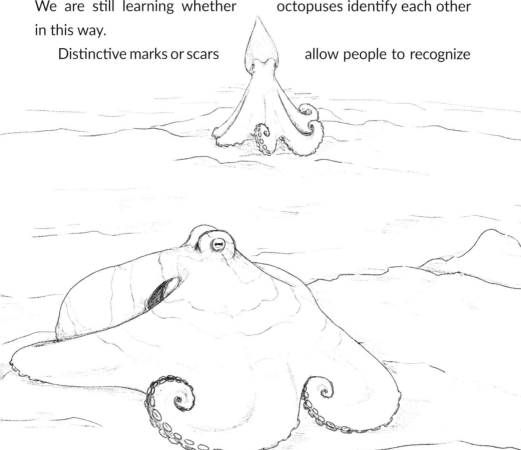

some octopuses as individuals. My collaborator Peter Godfrey-Smith noted particular distinct and recurring shapes within the changing body-pattern displays of the gloomy octopuses. One year a female had papillae with white tips under the eyes that distinguished her from other octopuses. Another had a unique peanut-shaped frontal white spot. Some octopuses bear distinct scars. In one video, we recorded the moment when the Quidnunc was nipped on the mantle tip by an Ocean Leatherjacket, leaving a recognizable white mark. Damage or partial amputation of one or more of an octopus's arms are also common, as are various stages of arm regrowth. We recognized, at best, about one-third of the animals present by scars and marks.

When markings are not enough, sometimes we can also track individuals as they travel. The process is painstaking, and inevitably an octopus will leave the shell bed entirely, moving beyond the view of our cameras. Unless the octopus has distinctive markings, when it then comes on-screen from afar, we cannot be certain whether the arrival is the return of the familiar individual or a different octopus we don't yet know.

In these instances we consider hints. Did the arriving octopus come from the same direction that a previous octopus had taken? Did the arrival head straight to a recently vacated den?

Our limited ability to recognize individuals creates a challenge for our understanding of octopus interactions. Is Octopolis an assembly of neighbors that are all familiar with, and able to recognize, each other during a period of days? Or might the octopuses be limited in their ability to recognize each other as individuals, just as we are limited in recognizing them? Perhaps the octopuses are also uncertain whether an octopus approaching the site is a previous neighbor or a new arrival. But it would seem easier for the octopuses if they could recognize an established mate or an earlier rival.

Cephalopods do indeed appear to recognize individual people, although much of the evidence is anecdotal. However, in one published aquarium experiment, giant Pacific octopuses recognized individual caretakers who had been nice to them (the octopuses approached those who had fed them even when no food was offered) or were not nice (the octopuses would avoid someone who had brought a brush too close even when the person wasn't carrying the bristly stick).

Amethyst, an octopus in the aquarium at my university, took a dislike to me. She would aim jets of cold salt water at me when I stood close to the tank. One day, visitors were being introduced to Amethyst. Not in the mood for a soaking, I positioned myself with the raised lid—a clear acrylic panel—standing between the octopus and me. As she came up above the waterline where I was presumably in view, Amethyst jetted a mantle-full of icy water up *over* the barrier, which arched to hit me directly in the face. Once again, I was outsmarted by an octopus. That day, she squirted no one else in the group.

In another aquarium study, the common octopus recognized neighbor octopuses and remembered them, at least for a day. This study, along with one of the octopuses recognizing their caretakers, provides hints that octopuses recognize each other as particular individuals, but this remains uncertain. Most octopuses in the wild seldom encounter each other, so opportunities to use this ability might happen only a few times in a lifetime.

Observations from Octopolis suggest octopuses do recognize each other. In one instance, a female and male octopus occupied neighboring dens, with the female at the lip of hers watching events and the male out of sight down inside his. In the near distance, a third octopus—a presumed rival male—approached another den. The watching female immediately left her den and grappled with the rival male before returning to her den.

The rival male then came toward her den. But instead, this rival entered the neighboring den still occupied by the first male. A tussle ensued. The female reached out an arm to get involved, then a second arm, before the original male emerged up from the den, kicked out by the rival intruder. The evicted male backed off, but the female did not, reaching a third arm and a fourth in after the intruder. Then she entered completely into the den, where a second wrestling match took place. A long arm shot out of the den past the female, reaching for a sucker hold, and the intruding male pulled himself up into view. He struggled his way out of the den, but the female held onto him with one or more arms, getting dragged from the hole as the male moved. One of her arms wrapped under his mantle, seeking a gill slit. She attempted the constriction grip, a killing hold in octopus battles.

The rival male dragged himself backward across the shells, pulling the female after him. When she was stretched taut, she released him and then scooted back to her own den. Moments later, the evicted original male also scuttled back into his den. The female offered the returning male a touch on the head with her second left arm, and the two tussled a moment before settling down again together as before.

This account is not proof, but it suggests that the female did distinguish the two males and acted differently toward each. Perhaps her treatment of the two was based on the rival males'

size, the intensity of some display, or chemical signals. Females of many animal species use each of these to select mates. Individual recognition, where it occurs, can also be part of a female's tool kit in choosing her mates. However, merely making the right choice when interacting is not enough to show that animals recognize each other as individuals. We do not yet know how this particular complex interaction worked.

It is worth noting that the evidence for cephalopod recognition abilities is weak. Mothers do not recognize their young. There is no parental care after hatching. There is no known family recognition. Cephalopods do, however, recognize their species. They can tell whether others are male or female. They probably make decisions about one another based on size, circumstances, and particular behaviors. We still have more to assess with this group of animals. But at Octopolis, at least, octopuses do not seem to follow simple rules based on the immediate situation, such as "resident stays, intruder leaves" or "the octopus next to me is my mate."

Many animal species rely on recognition of individuals. Some birds recognize their individual neighbors by their voices. Dolphins have signature whistles that identify them individually within their social groups. Asian elephants know each other by smell, touch, and sound. Paper wasps recognize their nest-mates' faces. Recognition is essential to the formation of primate societies, to the pride or pack structure of lions, wolves, and other social carnivores. Individual recognition reduces aggression. Recognition can be the basis for a social ranking, returning to a mate, or forging alliances.

The effect of familiarity alone—the sense that "I know this individual"—is less helpful than remembering details of past encounters: recognition plus memories. To know is to have access to a bit of information. To remember is to recall a scene, to hold an event in memory. Remembering brings to mind an individual's own past with details of what was involved, where it happened, and when. Event memory calls forth a past moment of oneself.

Event memory was once considered a uniquely human ability. Verbal retelling of an event gives us unique access—in a way that is not available to other animals—to understand human abilities to recall past events. Event recall is a broadly defined ability that includes forming the scene, the sequence of events, your own place in the scene, and more.

The key features of this recall are that event memories are associated with a past time (that is, "recently" versus "long ago," or "on my birthday"), a specific location, and other event details (what happened). Western scrub jays put individual small food items in hundreds of hidden spots in the wild and return later to retrieve them. In controlled experiments, scrub jays returned to a particular spot (where) to retrieve insect items (what) only during the short time after stashing that the insects remained edible (when). If too much time passed since stashing a particular insect, the hungry jay avoided returning to that spot and instead retrieved seeds that stay tasty much longer than the insects.

Many animals have memory of this kind, referred to as episodic-like memory. That is, the animal has shown it remembers what, where, and when, but we don't know whether it does this by recalling the past individual event. Episodic-like memory has been reported for several mammal species, a few birds, and one species of fish. In addition, two invertebrates—bees and cuttlefish—show this aspect of memory. This what-where-when memory may not be the same as recalling a specific event, but it could be part of what is necessary to recall an event.

Animals that recognize other individuals can use their shared history in making decisions and forming relationships. The female octopus choosing between her original male neighbor and the intruding male may have relied on a history with each individual, knowing one to be trouble and the other to be agreeable. The octopuses in the aquarium experiment, and Amethyst—the one that squirted me—used their history with caretakers to make decisions about how they would interact with us. These octopuses encouraged some caretakers to keep their distance. They readily approached other caretakers—those who, in a word, were trusted. To trust in an aspect of the environment is to learn how it behaves, to have confidence that it will act in a predictable way for better or worse. Trust is built into expectations, and expectations are part of both recognizing types such as predator or prey and recognizing individual neighbors.

Do octopuses display individual recognition sufficient for trust? Do they use memories of a relationship in making decisions? It would be helpful for the residents of Octopolis, if they could, not to mistake the Quidnunc for another. Other octopuses might be content to live and let live, but the Quidnunc is not one of them. He involves himself with others at every opportunity. He is full of bluster and threat that, when necessary, may be backed by physical force.

At least one scholar has compared the relations of octopuses to those of nations. This brings us to the role that the dynamics of octopus behavior almost played in international affairs. In the tensest days of the 1962 Cuban Missile Crisis, Soviet leader Nikita Khrushchev was bringing nuclear weapons to Cuba. Over the previous four years or so, anthropologist Gregory Bateson had been studying octopus conflict in aquariums, and what he had learned from watching octopuses in close quarters was important. As the United States and the Soviet Union came to the brink of nuclear war, President John F. Kennedy needed to hear what the octopuses were doing.

22

OCTOPUSES iN DOMESTiC RELATiONSHiPS

IN OCTOBER 1962, THE COLD WAR BETWEEN THE UNITED STATES AND the Soviet Union heated up. The Soviets had placed nuclear warheads in Cuba—and ships carrying missiles, launchers, and more warheads were on their way. The United States needed to establish new rules to communicate with the Soviet Union that would not make the situation worse. This dangerous moment brought the world to the brink of nuclear war.

Gregory Bateson thought his studies with octopuses could provide insight to help solve this problem. Bateson understood that for birds and mammals, communication was rooted in parent-offspring bonds. But to understand the communications between nations, Bateson thought physical closeness, which he observed in octopuses, might shed some light. Octopus females tend their eggs, but once their offspring hatch, their job is done. Octopuses are also notoriously solitary. These facts drew Bateson's attention to their surprising willingness to tolerate the closeness of neighbors as a metaphor for tolerant relationships among nations.

Despite their solitary reputation, octopuses like closeness. Thursday was another octopus that my daughter Laurel and I kept in a home aquarium for a while. Thursday was eager to interact with Laurel. On coming home from school, Laurel would put her fingertips in the water, and Thursday would leave her den at the other end of the tank, scoot along the bottom, and then jet up to the surface for a hello. Even after feeding, she liked to hold onto Laurel, sometimes for as much as a half hour or more.

When I chose a seat in the living room to read, Thursday would often quietly relocate in the tank to the point nearest me. She would crawl up and down the glass in my line of sight until I paid attention to her. By contrast, when Amethyst

squirted me with water in the lab, she not only kept me at a distance but also metaphorically showed her dislike.

The communications between octopuses are not based on parental care or mating dynamics. This insight led Bateson to wonder how these same interactions might help nations get along. Bateson had done a study where he kept two octopuses in a single tank. Because octopuses could pose a danger to each other, this is seldom done. Indeed, some octopuses harassed their tank mate again and again. But if introduced to the tank at the same time, some pairs learned to coexist. These cases particularly interested Bateson.

In these more agreeable pairs, there were minor battles early on in which neither octopus was badly injured, a sort of testing phase. The larger octopus stole food from the smaller and drove it out of shelter. After a time, the smaller cautiously approached the larger—a dangerous move—but the larger then retreated. As Bateson saw it, this sequence established trust. First, the stronger octopus demonstrated strength. The weaker then showed its vulnerability by approaching regardless. Finally, and critically, the stronger octopus then held back and didn't harm the vulnerable octopus, as though showing "I can hurt you but I will not." From this point, the two octopuses could coexist without fighting and would sit close together, sometimes touching.

Armed with these observations, in the final and most perilous days of the Cuban Missile Crisis, Bateson wrote a remarkable letter to a mentor who could share his research with President Kennedy's Science Advisory Committee. He wanted to alert Kennedy's team to the parallels between the international nuclear crisis and the behavior of octopuses, in hopes of giving them an understanding that could help resolve the standoff peacefully.

The Cuban Missile Crisis was resolved within a few days of the letter being written, so there was little time for the US government to act on Bateson's report and no proof that it made a difference. Kennedy had set up a naval quarantine around Cuba to stop only the Soviet ships carrying weapons. Kennedy could have chosen to bomb the missile sites or to set up a full blockade of Cuba, stopping all food and supplies. Either of these would have been an act of war. The more restrained quarantine was a show of force—one that aggravated Khrushchev—rather than immediately seeking a peace with him. Bateson remarked that Kennedy had placed "trust" in Khrushchev's judgment: the quarantine might have offended Khrushchev, but it was an offense the Soviet ruler could choose not to respond to. That is, Bateson felt that Kennedy's quarantine of Cuba had provoked the Soviets in just the way one octopus could provoke another. Would Khrushchev break the quarantine and land the missiles in Cuba anyway?

In the end, Khrushchev held back from starting a war. Six Soviet ships containing weapons stopped short or reversed course before reaching the quarantine area. Days later, the Soviet leader agreed to remove the existing nuclear warheads from Cuba. An operational trust had been established, allowing coexistence.

Bateson's observations came from captive octopuses interacting in pairs. Some of the behaviors he described remain rare or unheard-of in the interval since his work. Still, where we find octopuses together in the wild, they are busily interacting with one another in complex ways. While some of these interactions escalate into battles and can be deadly, most are settled by communicating through signals and brief moments of aggression that fall short of all-out hostility.

Underwater, South of Sydney, Australia

Two gloomy octopuses in adjacent dens at Octopolis both faced in the same direction, toward the outer edge of the site into the void from where danger could approach. One was the Quidnunc. Possibly, he would monopolize all the females and drive off all rival males if he could. Next to him was a large female, just a half-arm's length away.

He reached toward her. She lifted an arm in response, perhaps in irritation at his approach. The Quidnunc pulled back. Then, adjusting his posture, he extended the third right arm, his mating arm. The curled tip of the arm unrolled toward the female and extended. She tolerated this approach. The coupling was now out of view below the rim of the den. We believe they began to mate. Still, the male's watchful eyes were raised.

At the far edge of the habitat, hazy through a few meters of water, another octopus approached from off-site. The Quidnunc left his mating and sped to the far edge of the site. By allowing this interruption early in the mating, it appeared the Quidnunc sired no eggs.

The approaching octopus fled back into the void. The Quidnunc stood tall and dark on spread arms at the edge of the site, swaying and leaning out toward the fleeing animal.

This was a distinctive pose, the same one he showed to the females returning from foraging. My colleagues and I informally call this pose "Nosferatu," referring to the vampire character from the 1922 German silent film.

The Nosferatu is a signal to another octopus, showing that the Quidnunc will stand his ground and not back down. Octopuses in this pose are likely to pursue another, and other octopuses know this.

They may pause or change direction when they see the aggressive pose. Nosferatu poses can be more or less severe. At its extreme, the pose is large, high, dark, and intimidating. When an approaching octopus matches the intensity of another's Nosferatu pose, these meetings may turn into physical scuffles.

Octopuses also use a different signal, which is a low pose and shows the opposite of the tall Nosferatu. This low display includes pressing flat to the ground, arms and web spread, with the arms curled into neat spirals. The mantle is low. The web and mantle display a high-contrast pale and dark banding. Octopuses using the low display do not stand their ground when confronted.

In another instance, the Quidnunc raised up to watch when he noticed an octopus on the edge of the site crossing to the other side in a low posture. The Quidnunc approached, a movement that also brought him close to a female in her den, interrupting her. She gathered a web full of debris and silt from her den and ejected it at the Quidnunc with a blast from her siphon. The Quidnunc now stood even taller, raising his eyes above the silt cloud to keep the crossing octopus in sight.

Noticing this continued attention, the crossing octopus displayed an increasingly low display, getting wider and flatter to the ground with more conspicuous coloring. But the Quidnunc was not appeased. Displaying a strong Nosferatu pose, the Quidnunc steadily approached the crossing octopus. Then the approach turned into a chase, with the crossing octopus fleeing in pale guise pursued by the dark Quidnunc.

The signals between the two male octopuses were not the only behaviors of note in the previous scene. A female gathered up silt and shells and directed them through the water at a male. This is throwing, which is a form of tool use and also a form of social interaction. Nonhuman animals throwing objects at targets is relatively rare; those that throw projectiles at each other, as these octopuses apparently do, are rarer still. So far, such behavior has only been reported among social mammals, specifically, chimpanzees, capuchin monkeys, and dolphins.

However, it is hard to show that nonverbal animals are aiming at targets, as they do not say so. Because taking aim is an internal intention, held in the mind, it cannot be directly observed. Nevertheless, there are visible clues.

Octopuses throw in three different situations. They throw away debris when den-cleaning, they throw away prey remains after eating, and they throw material at other octopuses nearby.

Throws within range of another octopus often look targeted, different from the throws after eating and while den-cleaning. Octopuses throw shells, silt, and occasionally algae. But shells were more commonly thrown after eating or when den-cleaning, while silt was more often thrown with shells and algae when another octopus was nearby. An octopus that throws near another uses greater vigor than when cleaning its den. Both of these observations suggest that throwing is directed at other octopuses. We also found that these stronger throws were accompanied by the octopus turning a dark color, which signals a willingness to stand its ground.

Targeting has a role in interactions between octopuses. Females throw at other females, and these throws often hit their target. Throws by males rarely hit another octopus. As shown in the previous Octopolis interactions, females also may throw at males. Such hits occur during bouts of signaling, mild aggression, and jostling. Throwing does change the target's behavior. A throw can bring the targeted octopus up short. A target may duck just before the throw is released, reducing or avoiding the impact. Sometimes the target raises an arm in the direction of the thrower.

An octopus that throws silt and shells may discourage the target octopus from approaching or disturbing them. For example, a female may throw at a neighbor that is den-cleaning and shoving debris from her den toward the thrower's den. The offending female may then interrupt her cleaning. A female might throw at the Quidnunc roaming the site if he travels too near, and he may veer off.

As I described in both earlier incidents, octopuses filmed in our videos almost always used Nosferatu and low displays when two approached one another. The Quidnuncs stood tall in varying intensities of Nosferatu in nearly every encounter, whether they were on-site or arriving from a distance, showing their willingness to stand their ground. Arriving females coming into view from off-site most often showed low displays to the Quidnunc's Nosferatu. These arriving females—often, we suspect, females returning home from foraging—switched to show a partial Nosferatu pose once they got close to the Quidnunc. He then relaxed his display and followed the female to a den. Neither the Quidnunc nor the female really objected to the presence of the other. Females already in their dens responded in the same partial-Nosferatu way to an investigating Quidnunc's Nosferatu, staying put, offering no retreat.

A male confronting another male was a different story, usually giving differing displays throughout an encounter: one in a Nosferatu, the other in a low display. Which male adopted which posture, however, depended on their history and circumstances. The Quidnunc was often busy, and repeatedly challenged males that persisted in approaching the site. These males showed the low display as they came onto the site in view of the Quidnunc. But at other times, some of these males would stand tall in a partial Nosferatu when interacting with another male that was not the Quidnunc.

At Octlantis one year, where the rocky outcrops are broken into three patches at distances of several meters from each other, each small patch had its own local Quidnunc. Octopuses, presumably male, that the Quidnunc evicted from one outcrop repeatedly approached that patch or the others nearby. They approached in low display only to be met by the opposing Quidnunc in a Nosferatu pose. Once their quiet approach was noticed by the local Quidnunc, these incoming males retreated to the edge of visibility to try again at the same or a neighboring patch.

In an interesting twist on expectations, some males in the dens on the edge of the site avoided such encounters by staying in their dens, where they went unnoticed by the busy Quidnuncs. These quiet males attempted to mate with females that denned near them. Despite all of the Quidnuncs' bluster and busyness, or perhaps because of it, Quidnuncs were less involved than these quiet males in mating attempts. It is worth noting, though, that these are daylight videos. It is possible that the daytime jockeying by males gets them dens close to females and that the important mating occurs at night. As our cameras do not record in the dark, and lighting the nighttime scene would create risks from predators, we do not yet know what happens between dusk and dawn. As night fell on our videos and data collection that year, I hoped the evicted males were able to enter dens again somewhere on the periphery of the patches. It is dangerous out there in the dark.

There is a surprising amount of activity going on at Octopolis and Octlantis. Each octopus arrives at the same location but finds different circumstances. The octopuses are adapted to be flexible as they meet these challenges. The Cold War probing of relationships, the signaling of intentions that reduce hostility, and the tolerance of coexistence can be seen everywhere.

Evolution has shaped in octopuses many of the foundations for complex relationships. There are even limited hints of empathy with octopuses. My students note that when they splay their hand on the outside of the aquarium glass, the octopus will come to cover their hand on the watery side, looking them in the eye. This type of moment was captured in the movie *Arrival*, when the human trying to communicate with the aliens places her hand on the barrier separating the human and otherworldly environment. On the other side, an alien splays its very octopuslike heptapod limb. In my own living room, my daughter and Thursday, the octopus, shared this same greeting daily.

That wild octopuses are sometimes found together in one area has long been known and explained by the patchy opportunities for shelter. Indeed, the examples in this book may all be regarded in that light. Yet octopuses together are still surprising, especially because of their reputation as solitary creatures. It is the sophisticated behaviors by which octopuses cope with each other's nearness that fascinated Gregory Bateson and fascinates me.

If you visit Octopolis in the Australian winter, there may be only one or two octopuses there. The population is seasonal and thrives in the summer. Because gloomy octopuses live only a year or so, each year the site is inhabited by those coming of age. Over time, the central metal object has sunk a bit, and it may eventually disappear. New sediment is deposited all the time, and the shells may be scattered by winter storms. Are Octopolis, and a few other similar habitats, short-lived places where octopuses are brought together? Are these sites temporary?

This book introduces around twenty octopus species out of hundreds, whose differences are worth examining. In Alaska, my students and I encountered a large octopus species no one had noticed before. This new species is related to, but genetically distinct from, the commonly found giant Pacific octopus. It looks different, bearing a frill around its mantle that is lacking in the more familiar giant. The previously unnoticed species appears at greater depths than does its relative and may be more often found on silty slopes. Possibly, as the warming oceans drive the giant Pacific octopus away from shallow coastal habitats, these two species will encounter one another more often in the colder Alaska deeps. Like this species, many octopuses have yet to be the focus of more than one or two scientific studies, so our understanding of octopuses is based on the few most familiar or most curious species.

We see the interdependence of social animals: chimpanzees or lions that are drawn to live together in family units, parents with offspring and siblings with cousins. No such forces act on most octopuses. Typically, the parents die as juveniles hatch, and the young are dispersed on the waves. Yet the concentration of shelter in areas of plentiful food sometimes bring the octopuses back into each other's company. Here then is another model of animals in association—not in the way of cooperating families but of independently competent individuals navigating the demands of living with neighbors.

These clusters of octopuses, perched at the base of marine cliffs or in temporary shell beds, also hang at the edges of our knowledge, visited for short periods of collection or study but otherwise half-legend. Rare or short-lived, these locations tantalize us with the potential of their residents.

Even alone, an octopus will still draw a crowd. A bustling center arises around them, of associates, cohabitants, and neighbors. These attract still others—those seeking shelter, the diggers and winnowers, and the schooling masses. Passersby appear, hungry or merely curious—the groupers, sharks, and their kind. As from another world, divers and scientists drop in.

During my last dive on the Great Barrier Reef, a charming day octopus spent her time with me as part of her entourage along the submerged slopes of Heron Island. My air was low; it was time to leave. She was still by then, tucked into a nook of coral bommie. I began my slow slide toward the surface as I mentally bid her farewell. From my rising vantage, the octopus was there but unseen, so perfect was her camouflage. She is with me still—so tightly are we bound in a world of beings like her, like me, in a community of fellows on our small, blue-pearl planet Earth.

ACKNOWLEDGMENTS

Alaska Native Peoples, Lands, and Indigenous Knowledge

I THANK THE *EXXON VALDEZ* OIL SPILL TRUSTEE COUNCIL FOR THEIR work to designate community facilitators for all restoration work done with Alaska Native communities that, in turn, provided a process for me to learn from Alaska Native elders. All my community visits from 1995 to 1998 were arranged and conducted through this process. I am also grateful to the University of Alaska Anchorage and Alaska Pacific University for supporting my participation as a Faculty Fellow in their 2009 Difficult Dialogues workshop on Alaska Native ways of teaching and learning and on working with cross-cultural differences.

Thank you to Mike Eleshansky of Chenega, who returned with me to the shores of Old Chenega. Jerry Totemoff kindly gave me permission to write about our searching for octopuses in Tatitlek. Thanks to Simeon Kvashnikoff of Port Graham for his contributions and for verbal permission at the time to take notes and write about our conversation one evening in his living room, and to Apela Colorado for her wisdom and discussions of my references to Indigenous cultural materials in my work and for permission to describe our conversation surrounding the story of the hunter and the octopus.

Thank you to Dee Pletnikoff (office manager), John Johnson (vice president of Cultural Resources), Tatianna Turner (cultural coordinator), and the Chugach Alaska Corporation for help reconnecting with those I worked with, or their families, in the Alaska Native communities. Thank you to John Johnson for discussing with me my account of Simeon Kvashnikoff's tales in Port Graham and for permission to retell Annie and Galushia Nelson's tales of giant octopuses near Cordova, which also appeared in Johnson's book *Eyak Legends of the Copper River Delta, Alaska*. I am grateful to Cheryl Eleshansky for permission to write about her father and my visit with him to Old Chenega and his account of the earthquake and its aftermath, and to Chuck Totemoff (chairman and president) of Chenega for permission to publish my portrayal of the 1964 earthquake and tsunami at Old Chenega.

Thanks to Alaska Native Language Center (ANLC), University of Alaska, Fairbanks, and to Professor Walkie Charles (director) and Leon Unruh (editor) for permission to use ANLC published content in my work, and for approval of my account of my language interview with Michael Krauss and Jeff Leer (Chapter 4). Thank you to the family of Robert Cogo (Robert and Chas Edwardson, and Skíl Jáadei [Linda Schrack]) for permission to retell the story of Raven woman and the octopus (Chapter 5).

Thank you to Michael Livingstone, Beth Leonard, Karli Tyance Hassell, and James Tempte, Apela Colorado, Juniper Scheel, and Peter Godfrey-Smith, each of whom cared enough to remind me where I had failed to heed the lessons I already knew regarding Alaska Native and other Aboriginal peoples and to encourage me to seek respectful permission to include their stories in writing about octopuses. Indigenous cultures own their stories. History did not begin with European or Russian explorations around the globe. Alaska Native people are with us today and continue to practice their cultures; they have not vanished. Remaining errors, omissions, and missteps are my own. It is my hope and intent to celebrate, respect, acknowledge, and credit the contribution of Alaska Native communities, and the Aboriginal peoples and lands of Jervis Bay,

Australia, and the Vezo people of Andavadoaka, Madagascar, to my own experiences understanding octopuses.

I have tried to relate the stories from other cultures as I find them, but I've told them in my own words rather than take verbatim quotations from sources. I hope to honor the storytelling tradition and story work that relates a given story to my own and each reader's experiences, with contextual references that are specific to octopuses, rather than treating traditional story translations as linear or westernized plots. Therefore my retelling of these cultural stories should be uniquely meant for the intended readers of this book. However, the retelling necessarily blends my own style with that of the culture from which the story is drawn.

I relied on published translations or English-speaking narrators for all stories; errors of translation and Western adaptation no doubt are present, including my own divergence from source text. Sources are acknowledged throughout. I comment on the cultural role of these stories only in the words of the Native Alaskans and the Aboriginal people I worked with in the context of a given story. Inevitably, however, the cultural worldview of the source culture is obscured, misrepresented, or lost in translation to English. I see the stories and their meanings through my own light, and I relate those here in working with octopuses.

Research Teams

Thank you to the wonderful students, whose keen interest and bubbling enthusiasm result in many great conversations about octopuses and the things they do. A special thank-you to the many student aquarists, the fall aquarium biology classes, and graduate student coordinators of the aquarium lab at Alaska Pacific University for the assistance with animal care.

Thank you also to Captain N. Oppen of the research vessel *Tempest* for his professionalism, hard work, dedication to the long-term success of these surveys, and good humor in the field, and to fellow researchers T. L. S. Vincent, students of the annual summer octopus expeditions from 2001 to 2016 at Alaska Pacific University, and to all my dive buddies for their underwater professionalism, companionship, and good cheer.

In Australia, I am indebted to Matt Lawrence, who discovered Octopolis and provides inspiration and logistical improvements to all our work in Jervis Bay; to Martin Hing and Kylie Brown, who discovered Octlantis; to Peter Godfrey-Smith, who first invited me to visit the site; and to Stefan Linquist and Stephanie Chancellor for all the conversations about octopuses and for their good company and contributions in the field.

In Mo'orea, I thank Jennifer Mather, Tatiana Leite, and Keely Langford for inviting me to join their research team, sharing different approaches to the same questions, and for being collaborators with me.

I thank Blue Ventures, Charlie Gough, Bris, and the Madagascar research team for my opportunity to work in Andavadoaka, for reviewing the chapter on Velondriake, and for permission to write about Bris's underwater search for the trout.

Writing

Thank you to the Anchorage Title Wave Writers without Titles, who commented on early drafts of this book and provided a test audience: Celeste Borchardt, Lizzie Newell, Aileen Holthaus, Richard Herron, Les Tubman, and Mary Edmunds. Other readers of early drafts also offered suggestions for improvements, including Juniper, Laurel, Edward, and Griffin Scheel and Peter Godfrey-Smith, as well as my editors at W. W. Norton, John Glusman and (for the young readers edition) Kristin Allard.

Thank you to Tania Vincent, who participated in many years of the field work in Prince William Sound and planned with me the first conception that would eventually lead to this book. I am also grateful to Sy Montgomery, who read the early work and pushed me toward publishing, including recommending me to my agent and urging me to get started on the project after my documentary with PBS and the BBC was released. I thank my agent Leslie Meredith, who encouraged me to revise my book proposal and who found interested publishers to consider my work.

Many people helped me chase down facts or consider how to present the science of octopuses. Thank you especially to those who answered questions or reviewed earlier drafts of chapters: Eric Chudler (neurons), Dominic Sivitilli (neurobiology), Terri Sheridan, Vanessa Delnavez, and Richard Smalldon at the Santa Barbara Museum of Natural History; Marla Daily at the Santa Cruz Island Foundation (size records of large octopuses); and Charlie Gough of Blue Ventures (Madagascar). The book is better for their help; the remaining errors are my own. I am grateful to the cephalopod research community for being fascinating, welcoming, and energizing professional colleagues; it has been a great pleasure to associate with this community over the course of my career.

I am especially indebted to my lifelong and closest friends RLB and GSIII and to my family. Throughout my career, they have been my closest intellectual companions outside the academic world. They have kept me at home (to the extent I am) in the nonspecialist world, and been my companions exploring beauty's ultra-fringe.

GLOSSARY

aggression Behavior that intimidates or harms another animal. Aggressive octopuses may be defending themselves, fighting over a den, trying to drive off an unwanted intruder or rival, attempting to mate or discourage mating, or trying to eat a smaller octopus.

arms (of octopus) Octopuses have eight arms, each lined with two rows of suckers, although there are three smaller taxonomic groups of octopus species with only one row of suckers per arm. The arms surround the mouth. They are used for positioning the suckers, crawling, walking, holding and manipulating objects, searching for and capturing prey, camouflage, touch and distance chemical sensing (similar to taste and smell in humans), signaling, and grappling or fighting. See figure on page 29.

axial nerve One of eight nerve cords, each a bit like the human spinal cord, that consists of a series of ganglia down the center line (axis) of each octopus arm. Smaller nerves from the axial ganglia communicate with the ganglia of skin, muscles, and suckers along the arm. See also *ganglia*, *arms*.

beak (of octopus) A hard mouthpart of octopuses, used in consuming prey. The octopus beak is like a parrot's beak but more completely surrounded by muscle and not normally visible. The beak is typically worn blunt from action against the hard-shell parts of clams and crabs. See figure on page 70.

binocular (vision or depth perception) The ability of some animals (including humans) to view a single object at the same time from both eyes. Binocular vision occurs when the field of view of each eye greatly overlaps that of the other, so that most objects are seen from both eyes. The difference between the two images is one way animals perceive distance, which provides a sense of depth. Octopuses do not have much binocular vision and use other processes for their visual sense of depth.

bioluminescence The emission of visible light by a living organism, such as the glow of fireflies at night.

biopsy A sample of body tissue (such as muscle or skin) taken from a living animal for examination or study, or the process of taking that sample. Other methods for many studies now include sampling the mucus octopuses secrete, the sucker disks they shed, or their feces. These methods allow sampling without injuring the animal to take tissue.

bivalve Having a shell of two hinged valves. This property gave the name to class Bivalvia, one of the major diverse groups of animals within the animal phylum Mollusca, which also includes the chitons (Polyplacophora); the snails, slugs, and nudibranchs (Gastropoda); and the nautiluses, squids, cuttlefish, octopuses, and relatives (Cephalopoda). See also *mollusk, cephalopod.*

camouflage Appearances that conceal by fooling the senses. Octopuses hide by changing the color patterns displayed on their skin. They can also change their skin texture as well as their body posture and behavior to resemble nearby objects, such as kelp or coral.

cannibalism Feeding on another of the same species. Many marine species have very small young that feed on the plankton on smaller organisms. As these smallest young grow, they may in turn feed on smaller individuals of their own species. For this reason, cannibalism is common among aquatic and marine fish and invertebrates compared to its occurrence among terrestrial animals.

cephalopod One of the major groups of animals within the animal phylum Mollusca that are characterized by eight, ten, or more prehensile arms or tentacles closely associated with the head. Cephalopods are free-swimming animals. In modern, still-living forms, a shell is generally absent (as for octopuses) or internal (as for squids and cuttlefishes). Nautiluses are the exception with a coiled, chambered shell. See also *mollusk, bivalve*.

Colossal Octopus The common name assigned to *Octopus giganteus*, a species of octopus mistakenly named based on photos of a large carcass that washed ashore on a Florida beach during a storm in 1896. However, the carcass was later identified as the badly eroded remains of a whale; the scientist was mistaken, and the Colossal Octopus (unfortunately) doesn't exist.

crustacean A phylum of animals that have segmented bodies and jointed legs, including barnacles, copepods and mysids (plankton), isopods (pill bugs), amphipods (sand fleas), and decapods (shrimps and crabs).

cuttlefish A group of cephalopods that have an internal shell that contains gases to regulate buoyancy. The shell is called a cuttlebone and is sold in pet stores as a source of calcium for birds. Cuttlefish have an oval body rimmed with fins and eight arms as well as two tentacles used for prey capture. The fins are used for swimming and turning.

den-cleaning A behavior of octopuses in which they remove sand, shells, remains from meals, or other materials from the den, bringing it to the mouth of the den or beyond and expelling it.

devilfish A synonym for octopus that has fallen out of common use since the 1920s. Manta rays also used to be called devilfish, so be careful in older works to distinguish what kind of "devilfish" was involved.

event memory A memory in which a particular episode (the event) is recalled. People often tell of the event as though remembering it were a bit like reliving it, so that what happened, where it happened, and when it happened are reexperienced in memory. Scientists can show through carefully designed experiments that animals can remember what, where, and when, but the animals cannot tell us whether recalling what, where, and when also involves *reexperiencing* them. Thus, for animals, behavioral scientists speak of "event-like memory."

fishery An industry or activity of catching fish or other aquatic animals, including octopuses.

food chain A sequence of links from a biological energy source through successive predators. Thus phytoplankton is at the base of a marine food chain: a clam might filter the phytoplankton from the water and eat it; an octopus eats the clam; a sea otter might eat the octopus; and a killer whale (the apex predator, at the top of the chain) eats the otter. These links from phytoplankton to killer whale make up a food chain. There are many different food chains in the ocean, often crossing and intersecting in complex ways so that ecologists also speak of a *food web*.

food web Diverse, interlocking links between predators and their prey, such that a single food chain cannot describe what eats what. For example, an octopus will eat several different species of crabs, some of which feed on barnacles and others on kelp. Barnacles not only eat phytoplankton but also zooplankton, so that the biological energy eaten by the octopus has come from phytoplankton not only through a clam (see *food chain*), but also through zooplankton to a barnacle to a crab, and from kelp to a different crab. The flow of energy is thus not along one path (a chain) but through many (a web).

ganglia A cluster of nerve cells, located outside the brain, that performs a particular role.

gill/gill slit The respiratory organ of an aquatic or marine animal that extracts oxygen from the water. Mollusks have a unique type of gill called a ctenidium that resembles a comb. Octopuses draw water in to pass over their gills through two muscular gill slits at the forward edge of the mantle where the mantle attaches to the head.

head (of octopus) A major body section and the location of the brain and important organs of sense (eyes) and prey capture (mouth). Not all animals have heads; clams, for example, lack them. The head of an octopus is located in the middle of the body, between the mantle (holding the body organs) and the arm crown (surrounding the mouth). See figure on page 31.

ink sac The organ inside an octopus, squid, or cuttlefish where ink is stored, to be discharged as needed.

intertidal The region of the ocean located between the high tide and the low tide. The intertidal region is emerged (out of water) during low tide and submerged (underwater) during high tide.

invertebrate An animal without a backbone. Many familiar animals have backbones: people, mammals, birds, and fish, for example. However, backbones are found only in one group of animals (the vertebrates). All other animals are invertebrates.

kelp Large brown seaweeds, especially of the order Laminariales. Kelp is a type of algae. Some species can grow more than a hundred feet long and form dense forests underwater. Kelp canopies often form four to six feet above the bottom or at the surface of the water, depending on the species.

mantle The dorsal (top) body wall of mollusks that encloses the major body organs, such as gills, the digestive system, and the reproductive organs.

The mantle secretes the shell of mollusks such as chitons and snails. In octopuses, the mantle is the large muscular sac that contains their body organs. The mantle can be contrasted with the foot of mollusks, which is the body part used for crawling, digging, or holding on. The arms of octopuses are derived from the Mollusca foot—which can be confusing, but only because the same words are applied to different body parts for people. See figure on page 31.

melanin Any of a group of dark pigments, such as are found in skin, hair, or feathers. Octopuses have melanin in the skin cells used for their body-pattern displays and can also secrete it into their ink sac to use when needed for escape.

midden pile/middens A heap of set-aside or discarded items. When octopuses are done with their food, they push or expel the remaining shells away. These can settle immediately outside the den and form a pile full of interesting information about what the octopus has been eating.

mollusk A phylum of animals distinguished by a soft body, distinctive gill and tongue anatomy, and often a hard shell. Octopuses (which lack the hard shell) are mollusks. The phylum also includes chitons, snails and slugs, clams and their relatives, and other less familiar forms, in addition to the cephalopods.

natural selection The process in nature leading organisms to be adapted to their environments. Natural selection occurs because a trait that has an advantage to individuals and that can be inherited tends to be passed on to the next generation and so appears more frequently in a population; a less favorable trait tends to be eliminated.

Nosferatu pose A nickname for a display wherein the octopus stands tall and dark, spreading its arms and extending its web. The appearance resembles a dark, cloaked individual, such as a vampire, and the name was drawn from a silent film–era German movie titled *Nosferatu*. See figures on pages 139 and 159.

papilla/papillae (plural) A projection of skin raised by muscles to create cone-shaped, spiky, or flat horns or folds that contribute to body pattern. See figures on pages 36 and 37.

paralarvae A baby octopus after hatching and before transition from living as plankton in the water column to living on the bottom as a juvenile.

Passing Cloud display A changing skin pattern in which dark areas of color begin around (below, behind, or between) the eyes and pass downward within a few seconds toward the arm tips in a moving band.

photosynthesis The process in algae or plants of building sugars and starches from carbon dioxide and water using the energy of the sun.

phytoplankton Photosynthetic algae and other life that drifts in the water column.

pigment A substance producing the characteristic coloration of an organism. Octopus skin holds many very small chromatophore organs, each made up of a tiny sac containing black-brown, red-orange, or orange-yellow granules that are hidden or revealed by the actions of muscle and nerves, allowing the octopus to change its appearance very quickly and to generate a variety of body patterns.

plankton All the various animals, algae, bacteria, and other life that drifts or swims only weakly in the water column.

polarized light Light in which the waves vibrate in only a single plane, typically created by reflection of the light off a flat surface. Octopuses can distinguish different planes of polarization of light.

primary producers Life forms such as algae that build sugars and starches by capturing energy from a nonliving source, usually from light by photosynthesis, although there are also chemical forms of primary production in the deep sea. See *photosynthesis*.

primordial emotions Elements of instinct that command an animal to one kind of action that meets an internal need and helps the animal survive and reproduce, including, for example, hunger (prompting the animal to eat), thirst (to drink), or pain (to pull away). *Primordial* means "first in order," that is, before any others.

pseudomorph False or deceptive shape, used in reference to the octopus-sized blob of ink a fleeing octopus leaves behind, a shape that a less-clever predator might mistake for the escaping octopus itself (a mistake that this author only narrowly avoided on occasion when following an octopus himself).

Quidnunc From the Latin for "What now?" A title for the role of the most active octopus male, who appears curious to know everything that passes on his patch of shell bed at Octopolis or Octlantis, and so investigates or challenges every arriving or departing octopus.

radula A ribbonlike organ embedded with very small teeth, found only in mollusks, that operates like a band to rasp against the surface to which it is applied. Octopuses use the radula together with their salivary organs to scrape or drill tiny holes through the shells of their prey. See figure on page 70.

rapid eye movement (REM) sleep The more active of two stages of sleep, during which there are movements of many small muscles, such as those that control eye movements. In humans, more dreaming occurs during REM sleep than in the less active sleep stage (non-REM sleep).

reef gleaning Collecting small food items such as kelp or octopuses during low tide from reef areas that are exposed by the low water.

respiration Exchange of gases, such as oxygen or carbon dioxide, with the environment. Animals with lungs do this by breathing, which refers specifically to air or a vapor. But life forms without lungs, such as most fish, use other means. An octopus expands its mantle cavity to draw water in over the gills and then contracts it to drive water out, and the exchange of gases occurs over the gills.

salivary papillae A nipple-like projection tipped with small teeth and bearing the duct from the salivary gland, by which saliva is delivered directly to the site of a shell at which the octopus is scraping a hole. The saliva softens the shell; the teeth of the papillae and the radula scrape the softened shell away. The saliva also carries toxins that will subdue the prey when injected through the drilled hole and loosen the connections between the shell and the tissue of the prey animal.

siphon A tube through which water is squirted when the octopus mantle is contracted. There is only one siphon, and the octopus can move it to either side or even direct it beneath the web from behind. Used for jet propulsion, to direct a blast of water at an irritant, or in propelling (throwing) held objects away from the octopus. See figure on page 31.

subsistence foraging Collecting wild foods for household use (rather than to sell).

suckers (of octopus) Two-chambered, muscular, cup-like organs on the underside of octopus arms that can create suction to hold to surfaces, pull or push to move objects relative to the arm, touch, taste (sensing of chemicals on contact with a surface), and smell (sensing of chemicals dissolved in the water). See figure on page 31.

terrestrial Of the land or earth, as distinguished, for example, from *aquatic* (living in water) or *marine* (living specifically in the oceans).

tide pool A small body of water that is left behind as the tide drops and that becomes completely submerged again as the tide rises.

tool use The behavior of holding and manipulating one object directed at or on another object or another animal, such as a chimpanzee poking a branch into a hole to collect and eat termites. Octopuses that gather silt and shells in their web in order to propel them with a jet of water at another octopus are using the thrown objects as a tool to change the behavior of the neighbor.

tsunami An ocean wave caused by an earthquake or landslide that displaces a large volume of water. Tsunamis can be very small if they are far from the original water displacement, but near to the disturbance a tsunami can be a catastrophically large and destructive wave when it breaks on shore.

vertebrate An animal with a backbone. These include mammals, birds, reptiles, amphibians, fishes, and sharks.

web (of octopus) A sheet of skin extending down from the head and connecting the arms over a portion of their length. The web may be partially retracted or extended and contributes to body patterns in much the same way as the head and mantle. The web can also be spread to envelop prey as an octopus pounces. See figure on page 31.

zooplankton All the various animals that drift or swim only weakly in the water column, but excluding algae, bacteria, and other nonanimal life.

NOTES ON SOURCES

A complete list of sources can be found in the adult edition of *Many Things Under a Rock*.

Introduction: The Inner Lives of Octopuses

Project Cannikin reported a seismic disturbance "body wave magnitude of 6.8." The blast temporarily raised the surface above the test site by twenty-five feet and permanently raised the nearby beach and ocean floor by four to six feet.

The Cannikin test and other Alaska nuclear tests and plans were controversial. These were nuclear devices larger than those detonated at Hiroshima (about fifteen kilotons) and Nagasaki (about twenty kilotons). The blasts beneath Amchitka, located along an active fault zone, might trigger tsunamis or large earthquakes or leak radiation. In 1969, these concerns led to the formation of the Don't Make a Wave Committee antinuclear protest organization, which within two years evolved into Greenpeace.

The weapons test and its aftermath remain controversial. The 2011 report noted here includes the results of our Amchitka kelp-sampling efforts: radiation levels at Amchitka were not above what the US Department of Energy considers a very low and acceptable increase in risk to human health outcomes.

Project Cannikin, Amchitka Island, November 6, 1971. Atomic Tests Channel: https://www.youtube.com/watch?v=1JJEPBLL4E8.

Miller, P., and Buske, N. "Nuclear Flashback: Report of a Greenpeace Scientific Expedition to Amchitka Island, Alaska—Site of the Largest

Underground Nuclear Test in U.S. History." 1996. http://www.fredsakademiet .dk/ordbog/uord/nuclear_flashback.pdf.

Hunter, Robert. *The Greenpeace to Amchitka: An Environmental Odyssey*. Vancouver: Arsenal Pulp Press, 2004.

For a brief review of the question of hearing by octopuses, see Hanlon, R. T., and Messenger, J. B., *Cephalopod Behaviour*, 2nd ed. (New York: Cambridge University Press, 2018).

A pretty good summary of the perspective that octopuses were cannibals "with limited means to recognize their fellow beings" appeared in Mather, Jennifer A., Anderson, Roland C., and Wood, James B., *Octopus: The Ocean's Intelligent Invertebrate* (Portland, OR: Timber Press, 2010). See page 134.

Chapter 1: Starting Out in Alaska

The spelling of *tse-le:x-guh* was given by Michael Krauss and matches his usage in Krauss, M. E. (ed)., *In Honor of Eyak: The Art of Anna Nelson Harry* (Fairbanks: Alaska Native Language Center, University of Alaska Fairbanks, 1982).

The dAXunhyuu Learner's Dictionary uses the spelling *tsaaleeXquh*. Chugachmiut Heritage Preservation provides lesson plans for this Eyak vocabulary with this spelling (translating the word literally as "it stays under a rock") and with a recording of the word's correct pronunciation:

Learners Dictionary: https://knowledgebase.arts.ubc.ca/daxunhyuu -learners-dictionary/.

Lessons: https://chugachheritageak.org/ (see Food from the Sea and Honoring Eyak).

Pronunciation: https://eyakpeople.com/files/Dictionary%20Audio% 20Files/octopus_GL.mp3.

Michael Krauss died at age eighty-four in 2019: https://apnews.com/ article/70fb9e43f6da4d449f07a84d287275e4.

Chapter 2: Dangerous Giants

Here are two important sources for this chapter:

Newman, M. *Life in a Fishbowl: Confessions of an Aquarium Director*. Vancouver: Douglas & McIntyre, 1994. Portions of this book can be accessed online at https://archive.org/details/lifeinfishbowlco0000newm/mode/2up?q=octopus.

James Cosgrove's accounts of large octopuses can be found in Cosgrove, J. A., and McDaniel, N., *Super Suckers: The Giant Pacific Octopus and Other Cephalopods of the Pacific Coast* (Madeira Park, British Columbia: Harbor Publishing, 2009).

The term *Indigenous* is capitalized when referring to the original people of a land but not, for example, when referring to indigenous flora or fauna: https://www.sapiens.org/language/capitalize-indigenous/.

Chapter 3: Lost Homes

Until 2006, published accounts of the 1964 earthquake included first-person reports from Anchorage, Valdez, and several other Southcentral Alaskan communities but no first-person accounts from the village of Chenega. At the time I wrote the first draft of this account (1996) imagining the devastation of Old Chenega, I based it on Mike Eleshansky's account told to me at the kitchen table that night. I later revised some details using firsthand descriptions and video of the 2004 Indian Ocean tsunamis that hit Indonesia and Thailand.

Those same 2004 tsunamis prompted an effort to collect firsthand stories of the 1964 earthquake from Old Chenega. These were published in *The Day That Cries Forever: Stories of the Destruction of Chenega during the 1964 Alaska Earthquake*, collected and edited by John Smelcer (Anchorage: Chenega Future Inc., 2006). My imagined account of that day in Chenega has also been informed by firsthand descriptions published in that source, especially the recollections of Nick Kompko Jr.

Chapter 4: Our Cousin Octopuses

The quoted phrases about "extensive skin folds" and the sizes and shapes of papillae in this chapter were the key details from published descriptions of this species (aside from its size) that we had to go on for verifying identification. The most authoritative guides we had at that time included drawings but not photographs, and even the drawings turned out to be in error. Chief among those, and the source of the quoted descriptions, was Kozloff, E., *Marine Invertebrates of the Pacific Northwest* (Seattle: University of Washington Press, 1987).

Chapter 5: Octopuses Overrun

At least two plagues of octopuses struck the southern coasts of England, in 1899–1900 and in 1950. Some details as written here were taken from an account of the 1950 occurrence and fictionalized back to 1899.

Chapter 6: Global Octopuses

A detailed relief map of Prince William Sound can be found from Shaded Relief at http://www.shadedrelief.com/pws/. The map illustrates the retreating terminus (toe) of the Columbia Glacier, from 1978 to 2019. Satellite imagery can be seen courtesy of NASA at https://earthobservatory .nasa.gov/world-of-change/ColumbiaGlacier.

The oldest glacier ice recovered and dated from Alaska was thirty thousand years old; the oldest glacier ice in the Antarctic may be close to one million years old. The US Geological Survey provides answers to frequently asked questions about glaciers at https://www.usgs.gov/faqs/ how-old-glacier-ice.

Survival of *Enteroctopus megalocyathus* embryos, a southern hemisphere relative of the Alaskan giant Pacific octopus, drops 15 percent when the optimal temperature range is exceeded by even 1 degree. *Octopus maya* embryo survival dropped by 70 percent during current-day ocean bottom temperatures of around 30°C. With a further increase of just 1°C, no embryos survived.

Chapter 7: Octopuses Seized

A summary of the difficulties with large-scale octopus mariculture can be found in Franks, B., Jacquet, J., Godfrey-Smith, P., and Sánchez-Suáre, W., "The Case Against Octopus Farming," *Issues in Science and Technology* 35, no. 2 (2019): 37–44.

Chapter 8: Octopus Scraps

The more familiar species name *Cancer oregonensis* is currently (and correctly) *Glebocarcinus oregonensis*. A revised classification (Schweitzer and Feldmann, 2000) of the cancer crabs, in part based on discovery of new fossils, is used more among biologists now than when initially published. *Glebocarcinus* crabs probably evolved in the North Pacific and now occur only around the North Pacific Rim.

Schweitzer, C. F., and Feldmann, R. M. "Re-evaluation of the Cancridae Latereille, 1802 (Decapoda: Brachyura) Including Three New Genera and Three New Species." *Contributions to Zoology* 69, no. 4 (2000): 223–50.

Chapter 9: Octopus Tools

Our team described the telltale bite marks on crab legs in a publication about the field signs octopuses leave. The paleontological community, to my surprise, often cites this paper to understand marks left on fossilized remains, a utility I had not considered when writing this article.

Dodge, R., and Scheel, D. "Remains of the Prey—Recognizing the Midden Piles of *Octopus dofleini* (Wülker)." *Veliger* 42, no. 3 (1999): 260–66.

Chapter 11: Escaping Octopuses

I based my account of the moray attack in the imagined life of the day octopus in Hawaii on a video of just such an encounter, filmed in Hanauma Bay, Oahu. The moray in this video appears to be struggling with the octopus as much as the octopus is with the eel, as I describe in the text. The video may be found online at the National Geographic website: https://www.nationalgeographic .com/animals/article/eel-vs-octopus-video-hanauma-bay-hawaii.

Previously undescribed knots tied by the Green Moray (*Gymnothorax prasinus*) in Australian waters included the Moray knot and the Moray banana knot. Both have numerous body crossings, making them bulkier with more potential for the moray to apply tearing leverage.

Malcolm, Hamish A. "A Moray's Many Knots: Knot Tying Behaviour around Bait in Two Species of Gymnothorax Moray Eel." *Environmental Biology of Fishes* 99, no. 12 (2016): 939–47.

Wounds may be 80 percent covered within six hours of injury among fast-healing octopuses, although coverage may be only 50 percent or so among slow-healing octopuses. Much of my discussion of octopus wounds relied on these two sources:

Imperadore, P., and Fiorito, G. "Cephalopod Tissue Regeneration: Consolidating over a Century of Knowledge." *Frontiers in Physiology* 9 (2018): 593.

Shaw, T. J., Osborne, M., Ponte, G., Fiorito, G., and Andrews, P. L. "Mechanisms of Wound Closure Following Acute Arm Injury in *Octopus vulgaris*." *Zoological Letters* 2, no. 8 (2016).

Chapter 12: Seeing Octopuses

The firefly squid (*Watasenia scintillans*) has three visual pigments and probably sees color. This is a bioluminescent, open-ocean squid that normally lives below two hundred meters depth, except during the spawning season when it is found in surface waters. Perhaps its color vision enables it to distinguish between natural light and nearby bioluminescent firefly squid. Three other nocturnal squids (inhabiting depths between two hundred and a thousand meters) and the midwater gelatinous octopods *Japetella* sp. also have multiple visual pigments, again suggesting that color vision, where it occurs among cephalopods, may serve to detect bioluminescence.

Hanlon, R. T., and Messenger, J. B. *Cephalopod Behaviour*. 2nd edition. New York: Cambridge University Press, 2018.

Chapter 13: Reaching Octopuses

Details of Captain S. F. Scott's story appeared in the *Kendrick Gazette* (Kendrick, Idaho), March 18, 1904. See Chronicling America: Historic American Newspapers, Library of Congress: https://chroniclingamerica.loc .gov/lccn/sn86091096/1904-03-18/ed-1/seq-3.

A version of the blueberry story appears as "Woman and Octopus," in Krauss, M. E. (ed.), *In Honor of Eyak: The Art of Anna Nelson Harry* (Fairbanks: Alaska Native Language Center, University of Alaska Fairbanks, 1982), 99–107.

Octopuses coming ashore with agile suckers has long been part of human stories. In a five-book didactic epic poem on fisheries, Oppianus of Corycus (176–180 AD), a poet in ancient Rome, relates the love of the octopus for trees that flourished with splendid olives on the slope above the shore; octopuses are drawn from the water to close embrace with the tree before returning to the sea. Greek fishermen take advantage of this love, dragging olive branches through the water to which besotted octopuses are bound by desire and are thus caught.

Oppian, Colluthus, and Tryphiodorus. Halieutica. London: W. Heinemann, 1928; New York: G. P. Putnam's Sons. As described in Sauer, W. H. H., et al., "World Octopus Fisheries," *Reviews in Fisheries Science & Aquaculture* (2019): 1–151.

I was told the gem about the knife attack by fisherman and raconteur Vern Robbins many years after he survived his stab wound. Walter McGregor of the Sea-lion-town people told a story of a man being dragged below the water to live with the octopuses, related in Swanton, J. R., *Haida Texts and Myths, Skidegate Dialect Recorded by John R. Swanton*, Smithsonian Institution Bureau of American Ethnology Bulletin 29 (Washington, DC: US Government Printing Office, 1905; reprinted by Brighton, MI: Native American Book Publishers, 1991).

The moonwalk dance move was already a fan favorite at the Apollo Theater in New York, as performed in 1955 by tap dancer Bill Bailey. See it on YouTube at https://www.youtube.com/watch?v=y71njpDH3co.

Chapter 15: Knowing Octopuses

The study with target squares was Boycott, B., and Young, J., "Reactions to Shape in *Octopus vulgaris* Lamarck," *Proceedings of the Zoological Society of London* (1956): 491–547.

This intriguing finding is barely mentioned in the paper. Its significance revealing perceptual constancy is discussed in Godfrey-Smith, P., *Other Minds: The Octopus, the Sea, and the Deep Origins of Consciousness* (New York: Farrar, Straus and Giroux, 2016), 84–100.

Chapter 16: Dreaming Octopuses

The discussion about whether octopuses dream arose during the making of BBC Natural World, *The Octopus in My House* (2019–2020, also released in 2019 as PBS Nature, *Octopus Making Contact*) due to the work of director of photography Ernie Kovacs and director Anna Fitch. You can view the video of Heidi dreaming online at https://www.pbs.org/wnet/nature/octopus-dreaming-trept6/19376/.

My approach to the importance of animal dreaming was informed by a May 2022 book on the subject: *When Animals Dream: The Hidden World of Animal Consciousness* by David M. Peña-Guzmán (Princeton University Press). The book reviews the scientific evidence and philosophical perspective on the subject and concludes, I think justifiably, that, yes, many animals dream.

Chapter 17: Octopus Hungry and Afraid

A key source for this chapter was Denton, D., *The Primordial Emotions: The Dawning of Consciousness* (Oxford: Oxford University Press, 2005).

Chapter 19: Octopuses in Wild Relationships

Some of the ideas presented about Bearded Rock Cod were informed by discussions with Peter Godfrey-Smith and by the article "32. Housecats" on his blog *The Giant Cuttlefish*, http://giantcuttlefish.com/?p=3438.

Coral trout, groupers, goatfish, and other species may commonly follow foraging octopuses. I have photographed this behavior in Australia (coral trout) and Moʻorea (goatfish). The associations fascinate behavioral biologists.

Chapter 20: Gathering Octopuses

It is worth a note here about these vignettes that appear in each chapter from the lives of octopuses. All are based on actual moments I have observed or documented. The bouts of den-cleaning, collecting the sponge, and interacting with another octopus are related from a single video sequence captured on January 16, 2016, from a north-placed camera following our second dive. In a few cases, I have taken minor liberties in reconstructing such moments: this chapter's opening vignette of the female foraging is assembled from several different observations and moments. Specific details, however, occurred as related.

Chapter 21: Octopus Quidnuncs

The account at the opening of this chapter is not from any single moment but is composed of numerous instances across many video observations, as summarized, for example, in scientific reports cited in the adult edition of the book for Chapter 22.

In one study of three different octopus species in California, more than half of the animals had at least a portion of one or more arms missing. Some individuals had seven of eight arms injured. Octopuses generally are prone to damage to the front arm pairs.

Voss, K. M., and Mehta, R. S. "Asymmetry in the Frequency and Proportion of Arm Truncation in Three Sympatric California Octopus Species." *Zoology* (2021): 125940.

Paper wasps have distinctive yellow markings on their black-and-brown faces. Familiar faces are greeted nonaggressively with body contact, but when facial patterns were manipulated, wasps lunged at the unfamiliar face with mandibles open and were more likely to bite or mount the unfamiliar wasp.

Injaian, A., and Tibbetts, E. A. "Cognition across Castes: Individual Recognition in Worker *Polistes fuscatus* Wasps." *Animal Behaviour* 87 (2014): 91–96.

Cognitive scientists sometimes distinguish between *event* memory (a scene recalled as one occurrence) and *episodic* memory (an experientially relived scene about oneself recalled voluntarily from a single instance of memory formation). The stipulation of being "experientially relived," however, is challenging: absent a verbal report, there are no definitive behavioral markers of conscious experience. Animal behaviorists refer to *episodic-like* memory, and, for many, this is the same as event memory. For our purposes, the key feature of both is that remembering a particular scene (either as event or episode) entails a viewpoint of the self, located in space and time.

Scientists have discovered that the various similar scrub jays are not all members of a single species. Two species were once lumped together under the common name Western scrub jay (which is no longer standard): they are now called the California Scrub Jay and Woodhouse's Scrub Jay. The broader common term "scrub jay" encompassed Western scrub jays plus Island and Florida Scrub Jays. In the original report of episodic-like memory research (Clayton and Dickinson, 1998), the study subjects are described as "scrub jays (*Aphelocoma coerulescens*)," the species name now belonging to the standardized common name Florida Scrub Jays.

Clayton, N. S., and Dickinson, A. "Episodic-Like Memory during Cache Recovery by Scrub Jays." *Nature* 395, no. 6699 (1998): 272–74.

The "stay away" message of getting squirted by an octopus makes a good story. I have wondered, however, if octopuses have a different interest in squirting their keepers. Sometimes that first soaking from a large octopus is unexpected and gets a big response—a startled jump, shriek, or laughter: something interesting happens. Are octopuses in captivity prone to squirt the most reactive people in the room because it makes for interesting theater?

Chapter 22: Octopuses in Domestic Relationships

There were two key sources for this chapter:

Guddemi, P. *Gregory Bateson on Relational Communication: From Octopuses to Nations*. Berlin: Springer International Publishing, 2020.

Scheel, D., Godfrey-Smith, P., and Lawrence, M. "Signal Use by Octopuses in Agonistic Interactions." *Current Biology* 26 (2016): 377–82.

For an account of the octopus throwing silt and shells, see Godfrey-Smith P., Scheel D., Chancellor S., Linquist S., Lawrence M. (2022) *In the Line of Fire: Debris Throwing by Wild Octopuses*. PLoS One 17: e0276482 doi https://doi.org/10.1371/journal.pone.0276482.

Acknowledgments

The understanding of respectful use of Indigenous stories was informed by my conversations particularly with Apela Colorado, in asking and receiving permission from Simeon Kvashnikoff Jr. to relate portions of his story, and from the analyses of story work in chapter 2 of Drabek, Alisha Susana, "Liitukut Sugpiat'stun (We Are Learning How to Be Real People): Exploring Kodiak Alutiiq Literature through Core Values" (PhD dissertation, University of Alaska Fairbanks, 2012).

INDEX

Page numbers beginning with 184 refer to glossary.

Prince William Sound Science Center, 12, 14
pseudomorph, 82, 190
Puget Sound, 12, 17, 50, 64

Quidnunc, 158–59, 160, 165, 170–71, 174–75, 191

radula, 69, 70, 190
range shifts, 38, 40–41, 42, 47–48, 51, 176
rapid eye movement (REM) sleep, 121, 122, 123, 125, 191–92
recognition, 164–65
  in octopuses, 139–40, 143–44, 159, 160–63, 165
red octopuses, 33–37, 77
reef gleaning, 53–54, 55, 192
relationships, forming of, 137, 139, 144–45, 146, 159, 165, 175
respiration, 32, 130, 192

salivary papillae, 69, 191
scallops, 62, 90–91, 96, 100, 118, 140, 143, 148, 149–50, 151, 157, 158
  sponges in partnering with, 107–08
  vision of, 90, 94–95
Scheel, Laurel, 167, 175
Scott, S. F., 97–99, 100
scrub jays, 164
sea lions, 73–74, 75, 76, 140
seals, 21, 46, 76
sea otters, 21, 74–75, 76
Seattle Aquarium, 35, 50, 52

self, sense of, 112, 113, 118, 131–32, 137, 145
sharks, 14, 21, 46, 75, 86–87, 90, 141–42, 143, 150, 177
Shelter Bay, 29–30, 32
siphons, 32, 82, 144, 171, 191
sleep, 119–25, 131, 190–91
  dreaming in, 120, 122–25
smell, sense of, 74–76, 106
Smithsonian Institution, 13, 14
southern red octopuses, 136
sponges, 2, 63, 86, 107–8, 112, 118, 155, 156
squids, 4, 34, 41, 82, 112, 136
Steinhart Aquarium (San Francisco), 152
Steller sea lions, 73–74
subsistence foraging, 191
suckers, of octopus, 2, 28, 32, 61, 64, 66–69, 81, 86, 99–100, 191–92
  on detached arms, 131–32
  in exploring environment, 67–68, 101, 104–5, 106, 143
  in fights with predators and other octopuses 84, 85, 102, 162
  grasping of objects with, 101, 102, 117, 131, 132, 134
  gripping power of, 16, 67, 84, 101, 102
  in holding hands, 104
  in hunting and eating of prey, 68, 69, 70, 108, 134
  touch-taste receptors in, 105, 106–7, 108, 116, 144
Sugpiaq people, 10, 11, 18, 22, 98